By
GRACE
through
FAITH

MARK GARVER

By Grace Through Faith
ISBN: 979-8-9894852-0-8

Copyright © 2024 Mark Garver

Published By:
Garver Ministries
All rights reserved.
Printed in USA

Garver Ministries
Madison, AL 35758
garvermin@cwol.org

ACKNOWLEDGEMENTS

A Special thank you to my wife, Pastor Rhonda Garver. Thank you for not only doing the final edit of this book, but the wise counsel for all my life. Thank you for your love and support in every area of my life. I thank God that He brought us together to run the race He has called us to run.

Thank you, Doris Young, for helping get the Word out. You have brought my sermons and the messages God gave me in various places on this subject to the written page. I am grateful for your many volunteer hours that you spent making sure my voice was heard on this very important subject. May the Lord reward you openly for all you have done.

Thank you to all the staff who played an important role in getting *By Grace Through Faith* out.

You are a blessing to me. I have the best staff ever!

Pastor Mark Garver

CONTENTS

INTRODUCTION

There are many graces that God has provided for us through Jesus Christ. In the following pages, we will look into these graces and learn that when we walk in them, it will bring the glory of God. This is exciting! I will also show you that in order to receive God's grace, you must receive it by faith.

These are God's graces that we will talk about in this book:

- Saving grace
- Living grace
- Standing grace
- Serving grace
- Grace to be rich

Most people only know about saving grace, the free gift

of being born again and going to heaven when we die, which is the most important one, but once we're born again, there is so much more to know about His saving grace and the other graces that God has also made available to us. All these graces, which are accessed by faith, will enable us to live an abundant and victorious life while here on the earth.

I love this acrostic because it reminds me of what we should understand about God's grace.

G - God's
R - riches
A - at
C - Christ's
E - expense

To me, that says it all. God gave us everything at the expense of Jesus Christ. What an amazing God!

Grace is not something we deserved, nor could we earn it.

> *Romans 11:6 (NLT) And since it is through God's kindness, then it is not by their good works. For in that case, God's grace would not be what it really is—free and undeserved.*

Grace is free! It's a gift! It is undeserved, unearned favor bestowed on us by God.

It reminds me of the old car I had when I first met my wife, Rhonda. After we got married, we traded Betsy (yes, we name our cars) in for a better one. My wife is very sentimental; so much so that when she would drive by the car lot, she would reminisce of all the good times she and I had spent in Betsy going places. She longed to have Betsy again, but we didn't have the money to buy her back. Months later, someone bought Betsy and gave her to us as a gift. This was grace in operation! This person gave to us something we couldn't get on our own. Getting Betsy back wasn't based on anything we did, but based on the giver's character, desire, and ability to do it; and that's just how our God is.

Once, when my wife and I were away praying, the Lord spoke to us and said, "For this hour, understanding the subject of grace is very important." That's when I began to study God's grace more deeply, which led me to teach a series on the graces of God both in a minister conference in another nation and in my church. Now I want to share what God has taught me with you.

Why is God saying that grace is important right now? I believe it's because there's more that we, in the body of Christ, need to know and understand before we can fully walk in and do all that God has called us to do, both individually and corporately. My wife and I pastor together, and although we have taught on the subject of grace for many years, we know there is always more for us to learn.

We, the body of Christ, are called to be a city set on a hill, the light of the world, the salt of the earth, and I believe when we walk in the graces of God every day, not only will we have a victorious life and fulfill the plan of God, but it will also attract people to us, so we can help them and lead them to the Lord.

I thank God for this amazing grace, and for His mercy too! Both are important, and God has made them available to every born-again believer.

> *Hebrews 4:16 Let us therefore come boldly unto the throne of grace, that <u>we may obtain mercy and find grace to help in time of need</u>.*

This verse tells us where we receive His grace and mercy, and that's in His throne of grace. This is a real place, where we can go to fellowship with God and obtain mercy and find grace in our time of need. Although mercy and grace are very similar, they are not the same.

- <u>Mercy</u>: This word in the Greek is "eleos," and it means to have compassion, to show kindness to someone.

- <u>Grace</u>: This word in the Greek is "charis," and it means kindness bestowed upon one what they have not deserved, or stepping in after someone has done something wrong and totally fixing it, so there are no consequences for the person who did the wrong.

The difference between mercy and grace is that grace includes so much more. An example would be if a robber came in your house and was taking all your stuff, and you came home and caught him. Mercy would say, "I forgive you; I won't call the police; just put my stuff down and go." That would be great! Our God is like that because He is the Father of all mercies (2 Corinthians 1:3), His mercies are new every morning (Lamentations 3:22-23). I thank God for His mercy! We need this mercy, but we also need His grace.

So, what would grace do with this robber? Grace would also forgive and let the robber go, but then, grace would give the robber what they needed (money, food, clothes) before sending them on their way.

Mercy will forgive someone when they've done something wrong and not hold them accountable, but grace will go one step further and give them everything they need; and that's what God did for us.

By His grace is how God offers all His goodness to us! The mercy of God says, "Let's save them, and when they die, let's make a home for them, so when they leave their bodies, they will be with us." The grace of God says, "Not only will we save them and make a home for them with us, but let's heal them; let's bless them; let's make them rich; let's give them a life that is exceedingly, abundantly above all they could ever think or imagine; and instead of servants, let's make them sons and daughters, and heirs and joint heirs, so when I'm done, everything you've given me, I can give to them. Let me bless them with it all!" **That is Grace!**

God not only sent Jesus to cleanse us of our sins, but to give us healing, wealth, freedom, peace, joy, and so much more. God gave us what we didn't deserve and couldn't attain on our own. God is so good that while we were still all together unlovely, sinners, robbers, outside of the covenant, He stepped in and took care of what we had done by sending Jesus to not only take our sins and penalty, but to give us an abundant life while here on the earth. Jesus, who knew no sin, became sin for us (2 Corinthians 5:21), so God could give us everything.

God has done His part. It is finished. Now, it's our turn to do our part and receive what He has done. In the chapters that follow, I will explain each of these graces, their purpose, the importance of faith to access them, and the difference they make when we walk in them.

Chapter 01

GRACE & FAITH

Grace and faith always work together. Grace is God's unmerited favor, but faith is how we receive God's favor and His promises. Grace is God's side and faith is our side. In salvation, Jesus provided it, but we had to believe, confess, and receive it to be saved. In the baptism of the Holy Spirit, Jesus is the baptizer of the Holy Ghost and fire (Matthew 3:11), and the Holy Spirit does give us the utterance in other tongues, but we had to move our lips and tongue to do the speaking. With physical healing, God provided it, but we had to receive it, and then walk it out to receive the manifestation of our healing. Faith is needed to receive what grace offers and then, we must act on what we believe to see it come to pass.

Faith has never been a movement because those come and go. Faith is a foundational doctrine. Faith is what brings into existence what God has already provided; and because faith begins where the will of God is known, it is important for us to make sure we know His will, which requires us having sound Bible doctrine. Bible doctrine should always be based on at least two or three scriptures that support what we believe. It's also important when we read the Old Testament and the Gospels, to read them in the light of what the epistles say because that's where we learn about the new and better covenant that we have been given through the finished work of Jesus Christ.

Listening to sermons and reading books, including this one, are good and can enhance or clarify what we already know, but scripture, verses from the Bible, written by holy men of old, inspired by the Holy Ghost, the teacher, the revealer, the illuminator of truth, must always be what forms our beliefs. We should all be like the Bereans in the Bible and study the scriptures to make sure our doctrine is sound (Acts 17:11), and that we are following what the Bible says, not just what others are saying.

So, what is faith?

> *Hebrews 11:1 Now faith is the substance of things hoped for, the evidence of things not seen.*

The Amplified Classic says,

*"Now faith is the assurance (the confirmation,
the title deed) of the things [we] hope for, being
the proof of things [we] do not see and the
conviction of their reality [faith perceiving as
real fact what is not revealed to the senses]."*

Why do we need faith? Hebrews 11:6 says, "Without
faith, it is impossible to please God," or we could say,
"Without faith, it's impossible to receive from God."
Why? Because everything that God's grace offers must
be received through faith. "By grace" and "through
faith" are the two sides that are necessary to receive.
Grace is God's part and faith is our part. We must go
through the door of faith in order to grab ahold of what
God's grace has provided.

The word "through" means the access, channel of an act,
doorway into, or an entranceway. It's just like somebody
coming to our church service. They can't just wait
outside the lobby door and expect to be part of the
service. They must first walk through the lobby door and
then through the sanctuary door to be in the service.
Faith is our door, our way into His grace. If we don't
enter through this doorway, we can't get to the other side
where His grace (favor) is waiting for us.

That's why when a believer is struggling in a certain
area, it's generally because they lack the faith, or
revelation needed to boldly go to His throne to receive
the grace God has for them to overcome whatever it is

that has been causing them to struggle. That's also why two people can quote the same Word, in Jesus' name, but only the one who believes and has grabbed ahold of the promise, by faith, can access the grace needed to be victorious. It's only through faith we obtain the grace we need to resist the devil, live free from sin, serve others, run a business, have a career, raise a family, and live our daily life successfully. We must do it all through Him because we are not meant to do it on our own.

All of God's graces are available to every believer, but which grace and how much of it someone receives and operates in is up to them, because it's in proportion to their faith (Romans 12:6). It's the same with all of God's graces. Some people have only believed to receive the grace needed for salvation, so they will miss hell and make heaven, while others have grown their faith to received grace to walk in divine health, or in the ability to do well. That's why when the devil comes, some people can put him on the run while others fall into his trap. It's also why some find it easier to walk in healing, while others find it easier to walk in prosperity. It's always according to the amount of faith a person has received that enables them to access the grace needed to walk in victory in that area. Again, we can all partake of everything God offers, but we must first grow in faith to receive more grace, so we can walk in God's highest and best. That's why it's so important to hear the anointed

Word taught and to read and study the Word for ourselves, because that's how faith comes. That's how we grow our faith to access more of His grace. God is not withholding anything from us (Psalm 84:11), but we must enter into His throne room, by faith, where His grace abounds, to receive the grace He has for us.

God's grace is so good, and I wouldn't want to live without it. However, the revelation of grace that has come to the body of Christ, in recent years, has caused some of this teaching to get off with some saying, "Now that we live in the New Testament and are under grace, there's nothing a believer has to do because it's all up to God." This is a false teaching and has sprung up because those teaching it did not take what they heard back to the Bible and study it out to clearly understand what was being said. Instead, they took the parts they liked, put their own interpretation on it, and just ran with it. Scripture is not up to our own interpretation. Scripture should always interpret scripture. What I mean is, a scripture needs other scriptures to support what is being said

I've heard it said that this false teaching is "almost criminal" because they're not telling believers that faith is still required to receive all that God offers, which has caused some in the body of Christ to walk away from the truth concerning God's grace. This false teaching has also caused some churches to become one sided, either teaching all about grace, or all about faith. I've actually had people come to me and ask, "Are you a grace church, or a faith church?" This tells me they don't understand that grace and faith must work together. My response is always, "Yes, we are a grace church, and we are a faith church." I say it that way because a church is not supposed to be one or the other. Churches need to teach both grace (God's side) and faith (our side), as well as the full counsel of the Word, because it is by grace, through faith that we receive the promises of God.

The Holy Ghost explained it to me this way, "God, the Father, has freely offered grace to us, but humanity must receive it by faith." This means that the responsibility to receive His grace is definitely on us because God has already done His part by making His grace available. Then, once we receive it, we must learn how to cooperate with it.

This admonition (warning) I received from the Holy Spirit through a tongue and interpretation: "Be very careful as you listen, as you teach, as you hear my Word: that you divide it, but most of all that it is united."

God was saying that not only do we need to make sure we rightly divide (understand correctly) the Word of God (2 Timothy 2:15) that we hear, but also the one who speaks must do it in a united way. An example of this would be someone teaching on grace should also teach about faith because in scripture they are connected, united, so both must be taught.

Ephesians 2:8 For <u>by grace are ye saved</u>
<u>through faith</u>; and that not of yourselves: it is
the gift of God.

When someone teaches, "It's all about faith," believers can get very religious and try to make things happen in the natural, which will cause them to become very hard, like the Pharisees and Sadducees were in the Bible. If someone teaches "it's all about grace," believers can get greasy and loose, thinking they don't have to do anything, that God will just automatically provide it all while they live however they want to live. That's why we need to understand both grace and faith, and how they work together, so we don't fall into either ditch of becoming rigid or becoming greasy in our beliefs.

It's so important for believers to understand that walking with God is not a "do nothing" program (just sitting around waiting for God to provide everything), or a "works" program (trying to earn or striving to get what God says we can have). It is a "faith" walk, which means we are to hear the Word, believe the Word, build our faith, go to His throne to receive grace and then, walk in this grace by doing the Word and following the leadings of the Holy Ghost to receive what God has provided for us.

There is nothing we could ever do to make God do what the Bible says He has already done, so when someone tries to force a result, they are in works. Our faith will always work, but walking by faith is not a work. Speaking the Word of God is not a work, it is how we release our faith. Some people will bring up the book of James and say, "Well, James 2:17 disagrees because it says, 'Faith without works is dead.'" Yes, it does say that, but that word "works" is not the same meaning we have today. Back then, "works" meant corresponding action, so we could say, "Faith without corresponding action (to what we believe) is dead."

Let me give you an example. I grew up in Illinois, where it can get extremely cold. If one freezing night, someone whose car broke down knocked on my door wearing gym shorts and a T-shirt asking if I could help them, and all I did was say, "Be warm," and then closed the door on that person, that would be faith without corresponding action. I wanted them to be warm, but I did nothing to help them be warm, by inviting them into a warm house or giving them some warm clothes to put on. We can't just believe and talk our faith. We have to act on our faith too. When we believe something, we will not only talk like it's so, but we will act like it's so. Acting on our faith is our corresponding action and is what allows God to bring what we're believing for into existence.

I don't give to get God to bless me. I give because it's my corresponding action to what I believe. I don't confess the Word to make something happen. I confess the Word and act on it because it is my corresponding action to what I believe that activates the law of faith in my life and causes me to be blessed.

People who say, "I'm going to fast until God answers me," have gotten into works thinking that by fasting, they can make God talk to them, but God is always talking. Fasting is just meant to get our flesh under control, so we can hear what He is saying. We don't have to try and make God do something because He's already done it. What we need to do is, by faith, position ourselves to receive all that He has done.

Romans 4:3 For what saith the scripture?
Abraham believed God, and it was counted unto
him for righteousness.

Let's believe God and do what He says, just like Abraham did, so it will be counted unto us as righteousness.

Romans 5:5 But to him that worketh not, but
believeth on him that justifieth the ungodly, his
faith is counted for righteousness.

People who have a job expect to get paid for the work they have done. Romans 4:4 does say, "When people work, their wages are not a gift, but something they have earned," but when it comes to the things of God, a believer doesn't have to work to earn what Jesus has already paid for by going to the cross. We just have to hear the Word, believe, receive, obey, and walk in it.

That is how we position ourselves to receive everything that God's grace offers.

Part of positioning ourselves is knowing who we are.

> *Corinthians 5:21 For he [Jesus] hath made him to be sin for us, who knew no sin; that we might be made the righteousness of God in him.*

We are the righteousness of God in Christ Jesus! When we know who we are, we will approach God from our righteous position. John the Baptist knew who he was. When the priests and Levites asked, "Who are you?", he said, "I can tell you who I am not. I'm not the Christ." Then he told them who he was, "I am the voice of one crying in the wilderness. Make straight the way of the Lord" (John 1:19-23). The Apostle Paul was also bold about who he was. After he was elevated to the apostles' office, he said, "I'm an Apostle sent to the Gentiles" (Romans 11:13). Paul was not ashamed to say who he was because he knew he didn't make himself an apostle, God did. So, just like John the Baptist and Paul, we need to know who we are in Christ, and who we are not. We're not God, but we have been adopted as sons and daughters of God, and we have been made the righteousness of God in Christ Jesus. That's who we are.

God bestowed this righteous position, which we didn't earn, on every believer. The Apostle Paul called the Galatians "Foolish!", because after being born again, they went back to trying to earn their salvation through works. Let us not be foolish by thinking we can earn anything from God through works. Works cannot receive what only grace can offer.

God has made us righteous, not because of anything we did, but because of all that Jesus did. Some Christians think they're being humble when they say, "I'm just a sinner saved by grace," but that's a trick of the enemy. If the devil can deceive someone into thinking they're still a sinner after being born again, it will hinder their receiving from God because it will keep them from boldly and confidently going to the throne room to fellowship and receive all that God has for them. This is why it's so important to understand our righteousness and who we are in Christ.

Yes, we were sinners but once we were born again, we were made righteous. I remember in the early days of the church, there was this little boy, and people loved to pinch his cheeks and say to him, "You're just so cute. How did you get so cute?" His mom taught him to say, "I was just born that way." That's just how it is with our righteousness. We were just born again that way. Jesus took our sins, so we could be made righteous and receive all that this righteous position entails.

Knowing we are righteous will also help us guard against the enemy when he brings evil thoughts to us. Whenever the devil brings wrong thoughts to my mind, one of the first things I'll do is say, "Father, I've been made the righteousness of God in Christ Jesus, so I come right now to your throne of grace to receive help in my time of need." I do that, because at His throne is where I will receive the standing grace needed to resist these wrong thoughts. Then, I remind the devil and myself who God has made me to be, so I can say with confidence, "I am a child of God, and I am righteous. These are not my thoughts. They are your thoughts, and I resist them, and I resist you, in Jesus' name." When we acknowledge our righteous position and speak to the enemy from our place of grace, with the authority we have been given, the devil will stop messing with us in that way, because he knows he can't win against someone who understands and walks in their righteousness.

God is holding out His hand and waiting for us to wake up and walk in our righteousness in Jesus, so we will come boldly to His throne to receive His grace. If we never reach out and take this grace, by faith, we will never experience His goodness and blessings. If I took my wallet out and offered everything that was in it to someone, but they never reached out and took it, then my offer, no matter how magnanimous it was, would do them no good. In the same way a person must reach their hand out and take my wallet, we must also reach out with the hand of faith and take the grace that God offers.

If someone is having trouble taking anything that the Bible says God offers, it just means they need to grow their faith. How? By doing what Romans 10:17 says, "Faith comes by hearing and hearing by the Word of God." It's the only way to grow in faith. So, if you lack faith because you really haven't been reading your Bible, start there. Read it, and then study it, to grow and build up your faith to receive the grace you need for what you're believing. Then, release your faith by saying and activate your faith by doing what the Word says. This is how we walk it out to receive all that God has for us.

Chapter 02

SAVING GRACE

Saving grace is the grace Christians are most familiar with. It's the grace needed to be born again. God decided before the foundation of the world to make this grace available so we could be saved, not because we deserved it but because of His character, nature, and righteousness, and His great love for us.

Why did we need a Savior? Because even though Adam and Eve were made in the likeness and image of God, they had a free will, and in the garden, they chose to disobey, which separated them from God.

Romans 5:12 (NLT) When Adam sinned, sin entered the world so death spread to everyone, for everyone sinned.

Their disobedience brought sin and death into the world, which was passed down to every generation that followed. To reconcile us back to God, payment had to be made for humanity's disobedience, however, because we too have this sinful nature, we couldn't redeem ourselves, so God sent Jesus to be our Redeemer, to take our punishment for sin by dying on the cross.

Romans 5:15-17 (NLT)

[15] But there is a great difference between Adam's sin and <u>God's gracious gift</u>. For the sin of this one man, Adam, brought death to many. But even greater is <u>God's wonderful grace and his gift of forgiveness</u> to many through this other man, Jesus Christ.

[16] And the result of God's gracious gift is very different from the result of that one man's sin. For Adam's sin led to condemnation, but <u>God's free gift</u> leads to our being made right with God, even though we are guilty of many sins.

[17] For the sin of this one man, Adam, caused death to rule over many. But even greater is God's wonderful grace and his gift of righteousness, for all who receive it will live in triumph over sin and death through this one man, Jesus Christ.

Jesus, who was without sin, became our spotless lamb by

going to the cross. He paid for our sins by becoming sin, and then He put His blood on the mercy seat. By His blood, this one-time sacrifice, God was able to offer to the world His saving grace as a free gift, so we could be reconciled and in right standing with Him again. God offers this free gift of saving grace to everyone, but it's up to us to receive it.

> *Titus 2:11 For the grace of God that bringeth salvation hath appeared to all men.*

It is by His saving grace that God justified us.

> *Titus 3:7 That being justified by his grace, we should be made heirs according to the hope of eternal life.*

We have now been made heirs, or we could say, "By His grace we are not only heirs of eternal life in heaven, but we are heirs to all that salvation is and joint heirs with the Lord Jesus Christ while here on the earth" (Romans 8:17). Grace offers to mankind everything that God is and all that He has done. Through saving grace, we can be born again and be in the family of God.

God loves us and wants us. He has always been for us. He has never been out to get us. When I was young, I didn't understand that, so I would picture Him holding this big baseball bat, and if I did anything wrong or got out of line, He was going to hit me with it. I am so glad that I learned the truth, that God loves me and is good all the time.

If you have loved ones away from God, don't pray, "Lord, whatever it takes, or whatever you have to do, just get them." God is not in the "getting them" business. He's in the "saving them" business. That's why it's so important, especially with children, not to use God as a weapon to keep them in line or get them to do what we want them to do. Causing someone to be afraid of God will not keep them in line for long, and it can cause them to draw away from God. The Bible says, "It's the goodness of God that leads us to repentance" (Romans 2:4), so let's tell them how good He is and how much He loves them, and then teach them how to access all the promises of God.

God wants to save us, so we can be in His family, but it's not by our works. It's by receiving what He freely offers.

> *2 Timothy 1:9 <u>Who hath saved us</u>, and called us with an holy calling, <u>not according to our works</u>, <u>but according to</u> his own purpose and grace, which was given us in Christ Jesus before the world began.*

So, which family are you in? The choice is yours. There are only two families on the earth today. Jesus told the religious people, "You're of your father, the devil," (John 8:44). So, you're either in the family of the devil, or you're in the family of God. The good news is that everyone can choose to be in the family of God because God wants everyone to be saved (1 Timothy 2:4) but sadly, not everybody on the earth is saved and going to heaven. Why? Because salvation is not automatic. God gave us a free will, so it's up to us to receive the salvation He offers. We must choose to be born again, and God is so good that He even tells us in Deuteronomy 30:19 what to choose. He says, "Choose life." Choosing life is choosing Jesus!

> *Ephesians 2:8 For by grace are ye saved through faith...*

Both grace and faith are required to be saved. God's grace offers everyone salvation, but it is our faith that receives it. So, even though salvation is a finished work, it is not ours until we believe in our heart and confess with our mouth that Jesus is our Lord.

> *Romans 10:9-10*
>
> *[9] That if thou shalt confess with thy mouth the Lord Jesus, and shalt believe in thine heart that God hath raised him from the dead, thou shalt be saved.*
>
> *[10] For with the heart man believeth unto righteousness; and with the mouth confession is made unto salvation.*

That's all it takes to be born again. We don't have to talk God into it, although many have tried by offering up their good works, thinking they can earn their way in. Even today, people are still trying to use their good works to get saved and receive the things of God, but good works or good morals cannot earn what God has freely given, so if someone ever says, "I hope I've done enough good things to get into heaven," we know they are not born again. So, let's tell them the truth and get them born again!

Ephesians 2:8-9

[8]For by grace are ye saved through faith; <u>and that not of yourselves: it is the gift of God:</u>

[9] <u>Not of works, lest any man should boast.</u>

It's by grace through faith that we are born again. If we were talking with somebody not yet born again, and they kept saying, "Well, I see salvation is offered to me, but I'm just waiting on God to save me," that would be very frustrating to us because we know they don't have to wait on God because God is waiting on them. They can receive His salvation right now by doing what Romans 10:9 says, "Believe in your heart that Jesus was raised from the dead and confess with your mouth that Jesus is Lord." Once they understand this, we can help them by leading them in this prayer:

Father God, I believe that Jesus is the Son of God.

I believe that He was raised from the dead, and I receive Him as my Savior and make Him the Lord of my life.

If they really meant this prayer, they are now saved and forgiven of their sin of rejecting Jesus.

Until someone is born again, the sin of rejecting Jesus is the only sin God really cares about, but once they are saved and have become a child of God, He cares about all the sins they are still practicing and will deal with them about it. This is because He knows if they continue in sin, it will produce death and will keep them from walking in all the blessings He has for them.

God is the only one who can save, sanctify, and lead us into holiness. One of the things I kept praying out in the past was "Sanctification and holiness by grace." Trying to be sanctified and holy without grace is impossible and will cause someone to become very religious, which will produce bondage in their life; but doing it by His grace will produce freedom. I believe the Lord has spiritual doors for the body of Christ to go through, but to enter in, we must first be sanctified and walk in the holiness that Jesus has provided; we can only do this by His grace. God will always lead us to walk in sanctification and holiness because He wants us to remain set apart and free from the sin and corruption of this world. When we let the Holy Ghost reveal the Word of God to us, as we read, study, and are taught the anointed Word, it will produce freedom in us that will remain.

We are justified by His grace, and we have been made righteous by His grace.

Romans 3:20-24

[20] Therefore by the deeds of the law there shall no flesh be justified in his sight: for by the law is the knowledge of sin.

[21] But now the righteousness of God without the law is manifested, being witnessed by the law and the prophets;

[22] Even the righteousness of God which is by faith of Jesus Christ unto all and upon all them that believe: for there is no difference:

[23] For all have sinned, and come short of the glory of God;

[24] Being justified freely by his grace through the redemption that is in Christ Jesus.

In Romans 3, we can see that righteousness plays a big part when it comes to our faith. It was always that way even in the Old Covenant. However, back then they could not be made righteous, and that's why it was such a big deal when Abraham believed God and it was counted unto him as righteousness (Romans 4:3). Mankind was always trying to be righteous by obeying the law, but the law was only given to show them that they couldn't do it on their own. It is only by faith, believing Jesus took our sins on the cross, and then receiving Him as our Lord and Savior, that we are made righteous.

Romans 3:25-28

[25] Whom God hath set forth to be a propitiation through faith in his blood, to declare his righteousness for the remission of sins that are past, through the forbearance of God.

[26] To declare, I say, at this time his righteousness: that he might be just, and the justifier of him which believeth in Jesus.

[27] Where is boasting then? It is excluded. By what law? Of works? Nay: but <u>by the law of faith</u>.

[28]Therefore we conclude that <u>a man is justified by faith</u> <u>without the deeds of the law</u>.

It is by faith alone that a man is justified and made righteous, and not by doing the deeds of the law.

To keep walking in the "law of faith," we must keep hearing and doing the Word each day because it's not what we've heard yesterday that will keep us free, but what we're hearing and doing today. It's through the knowledge and revelation of Him that our faith will continue to grow. So, we need to let the Holy Ghost, the

Comforter, the revealer, who Jesus sent, guide us into all truth (John 16:13).

What we believe in our heart is what will enable us to walk in faith because Romans 10:10 says, "With the heart man believes…" The word "heart" in the Greek is "kardia," which means the center of us. It is our conscience, the voice of our spirit. That's why we must believe in our heart, the center of us, in order to be born again. There is no other way by which we can be saved; and thank God, we don't have to clean ourselves up before we receive salvation. We are to come just as we are,

Ephesians 2:5 <u>Even when we were dead in sins,</u> hath quickened us together with Christ, (by grace ye are saved).

Those who have been born again will find their name in the Lamb's book of life and will go to Heaven someday. John 14:2 says, "In my father's house are many mansions," so we know Heaven is a glorious place, full of blessings, and where the streets are made of gold; but God also wants to bless us right now, so we can fulfill our destiny and enjoy our time on the earth.

Once we've been born again, the next step is to walk in our salvation and all that it includes. The word "salvation" in the Greek is "soteria," and it means rescue, or safety (physical or moral), deliver, health, save, saving (on going). God wants us safe and delivered, and He will also rescue us and empower us to walk in health while we are on the earth, so we can live an exceedingly, abundantly above life. Also, the Greek word for save is "sozo," which means safe, to save, i.e., deliver, protect, heal, preserve, save (self), do well, and be (make) whole. That means our physical body can be healed and our broken heart can be mended; we can be protected and kept, do well, and be made whole. Being made whole means nothing missing, nothing broken. His blood covenant, through His saving grace, has given us all this. Everything that salvation provides is a gift. Healing is a gift. To be protected, delivered, and kept is a gift. Doing well and being made whole is a gift. He has freely given it all to us through the finished work of Jesus. It is God's gift to us.

I'm so glad we don't have to talk God into saving us, or filling us with the Holy Ghost, or healing us, or providing for us, or protecting us, or giving us all that salvation includes because God already decided, by His grace, to provide it all, and our part is to receive it by faith.

The Lord has been saying to me a lot, "Tell them who I am. Tell them what I've done." This is important because when we know who He is and what He has done for us, it makes it so much easier to enter in, by faith, and receive what the Word says we can have. Once we know that Jesus took stripes on His back so we could be physically healed (1 Peter 2:24), we can, by faith, receive our healing. Once we know that God protects us with angels encamped around us (Psalm 34:7), we can, by faith, receive His protection. Once we know He gave us His peace (John 14:27), we can, by faith, walk in His peace by keeping our mind stayed on Him (Isaiah 26:3). And once we know that Jesus became poor so we could become rich (2 Corinthians 8:9), we can, by faith, receive His enablement to prosper.

We have to know what God's grace did for us, but until we learn to walk by faith, we won't be able to receive what His grace offers. Grace is God's side, but faith is our side, and the more time we spend in the Word, the more our faith will grow. By faith, we received the greatest miracle ever and that was salvation, so by faith we can also receive everything else that God offers to us. The Spirit of God, the Holy Ghost, lives in every born-again believer, and the faith that we live, we live by the Son of God, Jesus (Galatians 2:20). And thank God for this faith by which we were saved and can now receive all He has for us if we will grow in the measure of faith we have been given and in our knowledge of Him. That's our part.

> *Mark 9:23 Jesus said unto him, If thou canst believe, all things are possible to him that believeth.*

God has made it possible to receive all of His promises, by faith. His hand is open to satisfy every living thing

Saving Grace

(Psalm 145:16). He gave us Jesus, so there is nothing He would withhold from us (Romans 8:32), but what determines how much we can receive is found in Romans 12:6.

Romans 12:6 Having then gifts differing according to the grace that is given to us, whether prophecy, let us prophesy according to the proportion of faith.

This says that the amount of God's grace we receive depends on the amount of faith we have and walk in. If I let my faith get weak, I can't grab ahold of my grace to receive His promises; but the more I grow my faith, especially in understanding His grace, the more grace I can access and walk in to receive more of what salvation provides. We need to continually be growing in faith, and this is how we do it.

Romans 10:17 So then faith cometh by hearing, and hearing by the word of God.

Faith does come by hearing the Word, but it's by hearing the rhema Cristos from the Word of God. Rhema is the spoken word and Cristos is the Anointed One, so when we receive a spoken word from the Anointed One, we can confidently walk in that Word knowing it will lead us to victory. When we read, study, and meditate on the Word, we open the door for God to give us more revelation, and then with that, a Rhema Cristos will

33

come.

Faith also increases by reading and speaking the Word of God, and then, when corresponding actions follow, we have positioned ourselves to receive from God. This is how we access and receive everything that God's grace offers.

> *Acts 20:32 And now, brethren, I commend you to God, and to the word of his grace, which is able to build you up, and to give you an inheritance among all them which are sanctified.*

By grace, God has given us an inheritance, but we must believe and receive it. God's grace offers us healing. So, we can either believe and say what the doctor says, or we can believe and confess what the Bible says, "By the stripes of Jesus I am healed" (1 Peter 2:24). It is by what we believe and speak that we will either receive the promises of God or receive what the world offers.

We can all have what God says when we believe in our heart and confess the Word, and then do what the Word and the Spirit of God says to do. No matter where we are or our position in life, no believer is excluded. God can take anyone from a dung hill and lift them up to sit with the princes of His people (Psalm 113:7-8). God didn't call us because of our wisdom or how great we are. He called us so He could make us wise and great in

Him.

Those who do not learn to walk by faith, will soon lose hope, and hope deferred will make the heart sick (Proverbs 13:12) because without understanding faith, we can't grab ahold and receive what God is offering.

By looking at our salvation scriptures in the Amplified versions, we can better see that all God has done for us is by grace.

Ephesians 2:8-9 (AMP)

[8] <u>For it is by grace</u> [God's remarkable compassion and favor drawing you to Christ] that you have been saved [actually delivered from judgment and given eternal life] through faith. And this [salvation] is not of yourselves [not through your own effort], but it is the [undeserved, gracious] gift of God;

[9] not as a result of [your] works [nor your attempts to keep the Law], so that no one will [be able to] boast or take credit in any way [for his salvation].

Ephesians 2:8-9 (AMPC)

[8] <u>For it is by free grace</u> (God's unmerited favor) that you are saved (delivered from judgment and made partakers of Christ's salvation) through [your] faith. And this

[salvation] is not of yourselves [of your own doing, it came not through your own striving], but it is the gift of God;

⁹ Not because of works [not the fulfillment of the Law's demands], lest any man should boast. [It is not the result of what anyone can possibly do, so no one can pride himself in it or take glory to himself.]

It is by grace we are saved! God, because of His love, goodness, and kindness, decided to provide salvation, so we wouldn't have to go to hell. God decided He wanted our bodies well, so we could live a long life on the earth. God decided He wanted us to experience all of His goodness now. God decided Jesus would become poor, so we could experience His abundance right now. He not only paid for our sins but made sure all the blessings of Abraham could be ours right now.

Receiving saving grace is just the beginning to receiving all of His other graces He has made available for us to live an abundant life while here on the earth.

Chapter 03

LIVING GRACE

In the previous chapter, I talked about saving grace, which is God's free gift of salvation. So, now that we're saved, we need grace to live each day, and I call this grace "living grace," which we also access by faith.

For a believer to consistently walk in living grace, it's important they see themselves as God sees them, otherwise, it can be hard sometimes, to know what's pride versus confidence, or what's humility versus feeling less than, so, by seeing who we are in the Word, it will help us discern which it is. My wife and I remind ourselves all the time that we're not any big deal on our own, but we also have to remember who God made us to be. A friend of ours who stands in the office of prophet will tell us, "You don't see yourselves correctly;" and this is something we do work on because for us to walk in the plan God has given us, we have to see who He has called us to be.

God wants all His children to walk in victory, and we can, when we see ourselves in Him and as He sees us. The ten spies are a good example of not seeing themselves as God saw them (Numbers 13). When they spied out the land, which was flowing with milk and honey, all they could see were the giants and walled cities, and they said, "This land eats its inhabitants." Instead of believing they could take the land as God said they could, they saw themselves as grasshoppers. The other two spies, Joshua and Caleb, saw themselves as God saw them and said, "They're bread for us. We're well able to take the land." Years later, Joshua and Caleb took the land as God said they could, but the ten spies, who saw themselves as less than, never got to go in. This shows us that when we don't see ourselves as God sees us, we'll not be able to apprehend the living grace needed to walk in His promises.

So, how do we change how we see ourselves? By using the Word of God as our mirror and letting it show us who we are in Christ Jesus. When we look into the mirror of God's Word, we'll see ourselves healed, with a sound mind, having everything pertaining to life and godliness, and we'll see ourselves victorious and complete in Him.

Jesus is the Word made flesh (John 1:14) and through

His death, burial, and resurrection, He has provided us everything we need for life and godliness (2 Peter 1:3) and to receive it, we must access and walk in His living grace, by faith.

Titus 2:11-12 (NKJV)

[11] For the grace of God that brings salvation has appeared to all men,

[12] teaching us that, <u>denying ungodliness and worldly lust</u>...

Jesus, through His Word, is teaching us to deny all ungodliness and worldly lust; and we can, by walking in this grace because it will enable us to walk godly: acting, talking, and walking like God. We should want to walk as God would walk because we were created in His likeness and in His image (Genesis 1:27). We are people of grace and faith, so we shouldn't be comfortable around any ungodliness. Galatians 5:19-21 gives us a list of what God calls ungodly, which includes homosexuality, adultery, fornication and so much more. All ungodliness is sin. We can see that worldly lust is increasing, and that's why it is so important to walk in this living grace because it is how we resist ungodliness. To those who say, "It's okay to live however I want and do whatever I want now that I am born again and under grace," will find that this scripture totally opposes that wrong thinking because it says grace teaches us to deny worldly lust. So, how are we supposed to live?

Titus 2:12 (NKJV) … we should live soberly, righteously, and godly in the present age.

This is how we are to live.

- <u>Soberly</u>:   Having a sound mind, being calm, steady, and living life cautiously with wisdom.
- <u>Righteously</u>:   To live right.
- <u>Godly</u>:   To live according to the Word of God.

Because we have been made the righteousness of God in Christ Jesus (2 Corinthians 5:21), we're going to walk uprightly in the light and not in darkness. When others look at us, our words and actions should show people that we're godly.

In a later chapter, I will talk about five of the warnings we are given concerning grace, but in this chapter, I want to talk about some warnings God has given to help us live a sober, righteous, and godly life.

Warnings are important. When I'm driving and see a warning, I immediately slow down. We all do, so we can see what's going on up ahead. Sometimes, it turns out to be a stalled car, or an accident, or it could be something in the road but whatever it is, we all slow down to see and know what we need to do about it. In the same way, when we see a warning in the Bible, we should slow down and really read what God is saying to us, so we will know what we are supposed to do. When we heed these warnings, our life will be full of peace, joy, and contentment.

Here is our first warning.

Romans 6:1-2

¹ What shall we say then? Shall we continue in sin, that grace may abound?

² <u>God forbid</u>. How shall we, that are dead to sin, live any longer therein?

This warns us that we are no longer to purposely continue to sin now that we're born again. It says, "God forbid!" That's a strong statement. Paul wrote this to the believers in Rome who thought they could keep doing whatever they wanted because God's grace would cover it. Grace was never intended to cover or be a license to sin, so Paul wrote them to straighten out their wrong thinking.

Romans 6:15-16

¹⁵ What then? shall we sin, because we are not under the law, but under grace? <u>God forbid</u>.

¹⁶ Know ye not, that to whom ye yield yourselves servants to obey, his servants ye are to whom ye obey; whether of sin unto death, or of obedience unto righteousness?

Again, it says, "God forbid!" Paul was warning them

that giving in to sin would make them a slave to it and would, eventually, lead to death because sin and death is a spiritual law. So, Christians who say, "I'm under grace, so don't put me back under the law," don't understand that the law they're no longer under is the law of religion, ordinances (rights and ceremonies) and doctrines of men, but there are still spiritual laws that must be followed, just like natural laws.

Gravity is a natural law, so if someone said, "Now that I'm a Christian and under grace, I'm free to jump off that tall building," we would think they were crazy. Why? Because even though they are free to jump, grace won't stop them from falling to the ground because the law of grace will not override the law of gravity, nor can we override other spiritual laws like the law of love, the law of faith, and so on. These are God's laws which must be followed.

Just like the law of grace won't override the law of gravity, the law of love didn't override the law of the Ten Commandments, it fulfilled them; and they are still in effect today because when we walk in love, we will not violate any of these commandments. The law of faith is also a spiritual law that must be followed because if we don't, we will not receive what God has for us. So, anyone thinking they don't have to follow God's spiritual laws because they are under grace, will soon find themselves not living the good life God has for them.

As I was meditating on how some believers are misinterpreting the message of grace and taking it to the extreme, the Lord said to me, "The reason people are gravitating toward error in My grace is because they feel condemned, and they can't get out of it." Then, the Lord said, "Instead of telling them what they're doing is wrong, why don't you just give them My Word and set them free?" What God said helped me so much because those who are struggling and misusing grace can only be set free and remain free by the truth of God's Word. That's why the Lord is giving us this warning because He doesn't want the law of sin and death to enter into our life.

Romans 8:2 For the law of the Spirit of life in Christ Jesus hath made me free from the law of sin and death.

Sin will always lead to spiritual death, separation from God, but it can also lead to the death of a marriage, or a friendship, or a job, or something else, but sin will always produce death. God wants us walking in His law of life, so we can remain free from sin and from having a sin consciousness, always feeling condemned. Those who are in Christ Jesus shouldn't feel condemned.

Romans 8:1 (NKJV) There is therefore now no condemnation to those who are in Christ Jesus, who do not walk according to the flesh, but according to the Spirit.

I've seen some believers take this scripture to the extreme and say, "It doesn't matter what I do because there is no condemnation now that I am born again." The problem with saying this, is they didn't read the rest of the verse that says, "There is now no condemnation for those who do not walk according to the flesh but according to the Spirit," so those who are still walking by their flesh will feel condemned, and God doesn't want that to happen to us.

When someone who is struggling to get free from sin, or can't seem to live or do right, is taught that it doesn't matter what they do because God loves them anyway, it will cause them to become very confused. Why? Because when they first hear it's okay to do what they're doing, it gives them a momentary sigh of relief, but it's just for a moment; then, when the law of sin kicks in and leads to some sort of death in their life, they don't understand what happened.

That is why Paul wrote, "God forbid!" He said it strong because God doesn't want His children to go down a road of destruction. So, when we see a warning like this in the Bible, it should be like a big flashing red light that says, "PAY CLOSE ATTENTION TO THIS!"

Another warning the Lord gives us is found in the book of Jude.

Jude 1:4 (NLT) I say this because some ungodly

> *people have wormed their way into your*
> *churches, saying that God's marvelous grace*
> *allows us to live immoral lives. The*
> *condemnation of such people was recorded long*
> *ago, for they have denied our only Master and*
> *Lord, Jesus Christ.*

This passage definitely goes off in my heart, like a warning sign, because not understanding what true grace is will cause us to receive wrong teaching from those who are making grace into something it is not. This scripture says that those who teach that grace allows believers to live an immoral life have denied the Lord, Jesus Christ because the truth is that once we are born again, living grace is so we can stay free from living in and practicing sin!

God wants us to be free from sin, but if all we have is religion and no relationship with Him, it will cause us to be too conscious of sin, which is exactly what the devil wants. Some Christians are this way because they have come out of certain religious backgrounds where they were told they had to do certain works before they could be saved or forgiven, while some Christians just naturally lean toward feeling guilty all the time. Christians who have a sin consciousness are always wanting to know what sins they've committed; i.e., sins of commission or omission, etc. Isaiah 61:10 says that God has given us a robe of righteousness, but those who have a sin consciousness are constantly looking at their robe to see if there are any spots or stains on it.

Those with a sin consciousness will not go boldly into the presence of God because they always feel condemned. That's why the message of grace is so important. It tells us we don't have to be good enough because God has already made us good enough by taking our sin and making us righteous. Once someone understands this, it will set them free, and they can then begin to live every day in His grace! Then, if something happens to cause them to stop walking in His grace and fall back into sin, 1 John 1:9 is there to get them out of their sin and back to walking in His grace again.

> *1 John 1:9 (NKJV) If we confess our sins, He is faithful and just to forgive us our sins and to cleanse us from all unrighteousness.*

Some Christians think that 1 John 1:9 wasn't written to the Christians of today, but the New Testament epistles were written to believers, so that includes us. If someone asks, "Does that mean if I sin, I still have to confess and repent, even after I'm born again?", the answer is yes. When a believer purposely practices sin, repentance from dead works is still required, but if we will walk in this living grace each day, it will keep us from purposely practicing sin. And once we repent, that doesn't mean we should keep a running total of everything we think we've done wrong that day, so we can repent of each thing individually each night. That's going back to having a sin consciousness. Just keep growing in the Word as you walk in the light of what you know, and the blood of Jesus will take care of any blind spots you might have, because His blood is continually cleansing us from all unrighteousness.

When someone says, "I don't have to repent and ask for forgiveness once I'm born again," it should cause a red light to go off on the inside of them saying that's wrong because God will bring conviction. Sin is not something to play with because the wages of sin, whether you're born again or not, is death. Playing with sin is like living on the edge, like people who stand on the edge of a cliff or a swimming pool. Those who do are just asking to fall or be pushed, so don't ever play with sin!

Romans 5:14-17 (NKJV)

14Nevertheless death reigned from Adam to Moses, even over those who had not sinned according to the likeness of the transgression of Adam, who is a type of Him who was to come.

15But the free gift is not like the offense. For if by the one man's offense many died, much more the grace of God and the gift by the grace of the one Man, Jesus Christ, abounded to many.

16And the gift is not like that which came through the one who sinned. For the judgment which came from one offense resulted in condemnation, but the free gift which came from many offenses resulted in justification.

[17]For if by the one man's offense death reigned through the one, much more those who receive abundance of grace and of the gift of righteousness will reign in life through the One, Jesus Christ.)

What this is basically saying is that because Adam fell, condemnation came and death reigned; but by the blood of Jesus, we can be reborn into righteousness. For me, I see it like gifts we receive at Christmas. Right after receiving the gift of grace to be saved, I received the gift of righteousness, which justified me and put me back in right standing with God. That's what His abundance of grace will do. His grace is meant to elevate us. It's like a beach ball floating in a swimming pool. As the water rises in the pool, so does the beach ball. That is what is supposed to be happening to us. As we stand in our righteous position and continually learn about grace and how it works, and then grow in faith, we can receive more of His grace to walk in, which will cause us to continually rise up.

Standing in our righteousness will enable us to access God's grace, so we can live free from the plans, plots, and tactics of the enemy. We are meant to reign as a king in this life, not over people, but over the enemy. Having revelation of our righteousness and walking in this grace is how we rule and reign. Christians who don't understand this are not ruling and reigning, they're just quoting scriptures and never seeing it happen in their lives.

When we start walking in this living grace, the righteous part of us will take dominance and rise up on the inside of us to train us on how to walk in our righteousness. The more we cooperate with this living grace and the more we walk in our righteous position, the more we will come to know what's right and what's wrong, what to get rid of and what to keep, what to bind and what to loose, what to allow and what not to allow. That's how we are supposed to rule and reign in this life by one Jesus Christ.

The devil is always trying to divide and conquer us by getting us to walk out of love or getting us into unforgiveness so he can keep us from taking our righteous position. Why? Because he knows if we get ahold of our righteousness, we will begin to rule and reign; and then he's done in our sphere of influence because we're not going to allow any more of his mess around us. We won't allow it in our house, in our body, or anywhere we go. Even the earth groans, waiting for the sons of God to be revealed (Romans 8). The earth is waiting for us to get in our place, sit down at the right hand of the Father in Jesus, and begin to declare and decree some things; but part of getting to this place is to receive His abundance of living grace.

Romans 5:18-19 (NKJV)

18 Therefore, as through one man's offense judgment came to all men, resulting in condemnation, even so through one Man's righteous act the free gift came to all men, resulting in justification of life.

19 For as by one man's disobedience many were made sinners, so also by one Man's obedience many will be made righteous.

Grace and righteousness work hand and hand. This is another reason we need a revelation of our righteousness. Before we accepted Jesus, we were sinners, but now that we've been saved by His grace, through faith, we shouldn't go around saying, "I'm just a sinner saved by grace." We were sinners, but that's not who we are anymore. Let's call ourselves what God calls us - and God calls us, "Righteous!" It's the same with all that the enemy tries to bring. We are not the sick trying to get healed, but the healed enforcing our covenant. We are not the poor trying to get rich, but the rich enforcing our covenant. By changing our words to line up with the Bible, we are calling ourselves what God calls us; "I am righteous, I am healed, I have the mind of Christ, I am more than a conqueror," and so on.

Jesus redeemed us from it all, so we could be healed, have a sound mind, be more than a conqueror, and so much more. It is because of Jesus' obedience of going to the cross that we get to reap all the benefits He purchased. Psalm 103:2 says we are not to forget His benefits.

> *Romans 5:20 (NKJV) Moreover the law entered that the offense might abound. But where sin abounded, grace abounded much more.*

Even when sin was abundant, it says that grace abounded even more, and that the law was given to show that they couldn't measure up on their own. It was God's grace and His gift of righteousness that put us in right standing with Father God again and gave us the same standing with the Father as Jesus has. So, no matter how abundant sin may be, there is always more grace we can access, by faith!

> *Romans 5:21 (NKJV) So that as sin reigned in death, even so grace might reign through righteousness to eternal life through Jesus Christ our Lord.*

When we were spiritually dead, sin reigned over us, but now that we are born again, His grace causes us to reign over sin and the enemy. It is through the righteousness of Jesus that we are now connected to eternal life, which is not just for when we get to Heaven, but while we're on the earth too! This grace not only made us righteous, but it opened to us zoe, the God kind and quality of life that we get to live now, while we are on the earth!

Galatians 5:1-3 (NKJV)

¹ Stand fast therefore in the liberty wherewith Christ hath made us free, and be not entangled again with the yoke of bondage.

²Behold, I Paul say unto you, that if ye be circumcised, Christ shall profit you nothing.

³ And I testify again to every man who becomes circumcised that he is a debtor to keep the whole law.

This was another warning Paul gave to believers who wanted to go back to the law. He told them if they went back to doing the law, that God's grace would no longer profit them. I still see people who mix New Testament teaching with the Old Testament law, and when they do, it always turns into a mess because that is not how we receive from God. We can't earn His blessings that way because no one can keep the whole law. It's impossible! The law was only meant to show our need for a Savior, Jesus Christ.

Romans 5:4-5 (NKJV)

⁴ You have become estranged from Christ, you who attempt to be justified by law; you have fallen from grace.

⁵ For we through the Spirit eagerly wait for the hope of righteousness by faith.

Any time we're not walking in the gift of righteousness, we have fallen from grace and are trying to earn our righteousness by what we do. That won't work because grace is the only door to righteousness. If we don't walk in the grace of God, we're not profiting from it, and are left trying to do it on our own. God never meant for us to deal with anything on our own, and when we try, we will fail. Why? Because without God and His grace, we are no match for the enemy.

The Lord has made it very clear that when it comes to sin, He doesn't want us practicing, walking in, or dealing with it because He knows the paycheck for sin is always death. But the good news is, we don't have to live in sin because we can walk in His living grace, which will keep us out of sin.

Romans 6:3-4 (NKJV)

³ Or do you not know that as many of us as were baptized into Christ Jesus were baptized into His death?

⁴ Therefore we were buried with Him through baptism into death, that just as Christ was raised from the dead by the glory of the Father, even so <u>we also should walk in newness of life</u>.

This newness of life is zoe, the God kind of life, and is what God wants us to walk in. How? Through faith in

Jesus. We were saved by grace because of what Jesus did, and that grace gave us righteousness, which gave us eternal life; and this eternal life doesn't begin when we go to heaven. It began the moment we were born again, so we could walk in the God kind and quality of life now, while we are on the earth. As we do this, His grace will keep us free from sin because, just like Jesus, we are dead to it, and alive unto God! How did we become dead to sin?

Romans 6:5-9

⁵ For if we've been planted together in the likeness of death, we shall be also in the likeness of his resurrection:

⁶ For if we have been united together in the likeness of His death, certainly we also shall be in the likeness of His resurrection,

⁷ For he who has died has been freed from sin

⁸ Now if we died with Christ, we believe that we shall also live with Him,

⁹ knowing that Christ, having been raised from the dead, dies no more. <u>Death no longer has dominion over Him</u>.

It says that death no longer has dominion over us. So, since sin has to do with death, that means that sin has no dominion over a believer. When it comes to sin, we should be dead men walking. What do I mean by that?

54

It means that we're alive to the things of God, but dead to the things of this world that oppose the Word of God. If someone is dead to something, that means they are no longer affected by it. So, since we're dead to the things of this world, we're dead to sin and free from it! If someone tries to offend us, or traffic is backed up, or something tries to get us to walk out of love, it has no authority (dominion), no effect on us because we are dead to it. We can rise above it and choose to be patient, to forgive, and walk in love regardless of what comes at us because anything having to do with sin no longer has dominion over us when we're walking in God's living grace!

Romans 6:10-14 (NKJV)

[10] For the death that He died, He died to sin once for all; but the life that He lives, He lives to God.

[11] Likewise you also, reckon yourselves to be dead indeed to sin, but alive to God in Christ Jesus our Lord.

[12] Therefore do not let sin reign in your mortal body, that you should obey it in its lusts.

[13] And do not present your members as instruments of unrighteousness to sin, but present yourselves to God as being alive from the dead, and your members as instruments of righteousness to God.

> *¹⁴ For sin shall not have dominion over you, for
> you are not under law but under grace.*

To get to the place where sin no longer has dominion over us, we need a revelation of our righteous position because it is from this place that we rule and reign. By walking in this grace, we will be able to quit yielding our body to sin and will no longer want to do the things we shouldn't be doing.

Romans 6:17-19 (NKJV)

> *¹⁷ But God be thanked that though you were
> slaves of sin, yet you obeyed from the heart that
> form of doctrine to which you were delivered.*

> *¹⁸ And having been set free from sin, you
> became slaves of righteousness.*

> *¹⁹ I speak in human terms because of the
> weakness of your flesh. For just as you
> presented your members as slaves of
> uncleanness, and of lawlessness leading to more
> lawlessness so now present your members as
> slaves of righteousness for holiness.*

When we let our flesh run wild, the scripture tells us that we're slaves to uncleanliness and lawlessness, which will lead to more lawlessness; but thank God, we don't have to live that way anymore! We can offer our bodies unto the Lord, and He will give us living grace that will cause us to yield to holiness.

Romans 6:20-23 (NKJV)

²⁰ For when you were slaves of sin, you were free in regard to righteousness.

²¹ What fruit did you have then in the things of which you are now ashamed? For the end of those things is death.

²² But now having been set free from sin, and having become slaves of God, you have your fruit to holiness, and the end, everlasting life.

²³ For the wages of sin is death, but the gift of God is eternal life in Christ Jesus our Lord.

Again, sin will always lead to death, but living grace will always lead us to righteousness, eternal life, and the zoe life while we are here on the earth! If we will let the Holy Spirit work in us, His quickening power will come and give us the strength we need to walk in our righteousness.

I have addressed several warnings concerning walking in living grace victoriously, but where does someone begin? By first knowing they have been made righteous then, believing for living grace and confessing they have it; when they do, this living grace will enable them to walk by faith and in God's law of love.

So, how do we walk in love? 1 Corinthians 13:4-7 in the Amplified Classic is the best definition I've ever seen of walking in love, and also, in telling us how to do it.

1 Corinthians 13:4-7 (AMPC)

[4] Love endures long and is patient and kind; love never is envious nor boils over with jealousy, is not boastful or vainglorious, does not display itself haughtily.

[5] It is not conceited (arrogant and inflated with pride); it is not rude (unmannerly) and does not act unbecomingly. Love (God's love in us) does not insist on its own rights or its own way, for it is not self-seeking; it is not touchy or fretful or resentful; it takes no account of the evil done to it [it pays no attention to a suffered wrong].

[6] It does not rejoice at injustice and unrighteousness, but rejoices when right and truth prevail.

[7] Love bears up under anything and everything that comes, is ever ready to believe the best of every person, its hopes are fadeless under all circumstances, and it endures everything [without weakening].

It's as easy as that, but that doesn't mean it's always easy to do. That's why it's so important to grow in the fruit of the spirit mentioned in Ephesians 5:22-23, "But the fruit of the Spirit is love, joy, peace, longsuffering, gentleness, goodness, faith, meekness, temperance:

against such there is no law."

How can we all get to that place of having the grace we need in what we do? We do it by faith. As we grow our faith, the more living grace we can access and walk in!

The Bible says that the just (Christians) shall live by faith (Habakkuk 2:4, Romans 1:17, Galatians 3:11, Hebrews 10:38). How are we going to get through the day? By receiving His living grace, through faith, to handle all that comes our way. We should live our entire life by grace through faith!

Chapter 04

STANDING GRACE

What is standing grace?

> *Romans 5:2 By whom also we have access by faith into <u>this grace wherein we stand</u>, and rejoice in hope of the glory of God.*

> *1 Peter 5:12 By Silvanus, a faithful brother unto you, as I suppose, I have written briefly, exhorting, and testifying that this is the true <u>grace of God wherein ye stand</u>.*

It is the grace God has made available for us to stand against the devil and his works, and I call that standing grace.

Receiving His standing grace.

Our doorway to this grace, and to all His other graces, is through faith. It is by faith that we go to God's throne and receive this grace in which we stand (Hebrews 4:16); but to receive it, we must humble ourselves.

> *James 4:6 (NKJV) But He gives [us] more grace. Therefore He says: "God resists the proud, but gives grace to the humble."*

It says that God gives this grace, and even more of this grace, to the humble and not to the proud. Why does God resist the proud? Because pride was the original sin that caused the devil to fall from Heaven. Where there is pride, there is destruction, which can result in a great fall like it did with the devil. When someone is proud, it's like God stretches His arm out and keeps them away. The literal translation is that He gives them a straight arm, so they can't get close enough to receive His grace. We don't want God doing that to us.

Some people like to sound humble and will say things like, "I'm nothing but a worm," or "I'm just a sinner." Although it sounds humble to say, this is false humility because those who are born again are not worms and are no longer sinners. We are now the righteousness of God in Christ Jesus, and we need to see ourselves the way God sees us.

So, what does pride look like? It's somebody who thinks they can do it on their own and they don't need anybody. They think they're smarter and better than everybody else. That is pride and God resists that.

When we think about ourselves too much, that's pride because when we become too self-focused, we're not God focused. Instead of trying to defend ourselves, we need to let God defend us. The Bible says that the battle is not ours, but God's (2 Chronicles 20:15), and that every tongue that shall rise against us in judgment, God shall condemn (Isaiah 54:17). Just take your hands off, give it to the Lord, and let Him take care of it.

Pride is something that we all, including pastors, have to guard against. It's so easy for a pastor to become prideful, especially when the people around them put them on a pedestal. A pastor, who is full of pride, thinks and may even say, "I don't need anyone. I got this. I can do this on my own. My church is the only one that matters, and everyone should come here, because I'm the only one who has the truth." This prideful thinking is self-deception and can put that person on a very bad path because Proverbs 16:18 says, "Pride goes before a fall," or we could say that pride is followed by a fall. We have seen that happen in the church through the years. Getting into pride is what the devil did, and we can see what it did for him. He had a great fall from heaven because where there is pride, there is destruction. Let's not fall into that trap. Let's remain humble, so we don't get tripped up.

So, what does it really mean to be humble? It's realizing we can't do it on our own. We need Jesus and everything He's done for us. He's our Savior, but He's also our Lord and Master. He's our everything. Humility is total reliance on someone else; for a Christian, that someone else is God. Admitting we are totally relying on God is true humility.

There are those who will say, "Total reliance on someone is a crutch, and it shows weakness," but it's just the opposite. When we know and understand who God is, and we see how much He loves and cares for us, and how much we need Him, submitting to God is a sign of strength.

You have to be humble enough to admit your dependence on Him; and when you do, He will give you more and more grace to meet every evil that comes our way. Being prideful, thinking you can do it on your own, will keep you from receiving this grace that you need because God resists the proud.

> *James 4:6 (AMPC) But He gives us more and more grace (power of the Holy Spirit, to meet this evil tendency and all others fully). That is why He says, God sets Himself against the proud and haughty, but gives grace [continually] to the lowly (those who are*

humble enough to receive it).

These "In Myself" realities are good confessions to remind us of our dependency on Him.

1. In myself, I am nothing (Galatians 6:3).
2. In myself, I know nothing (1 Corinthians 8:2).
3. In myself, I have nothing (1 Corinthians 4:7).
4. In myself, I can do nothing (John 15:5).

Thank God, we're not in ourselves anymore. We're in Christ Jesus! I'm strong, but I'm not strong in myself. I am strong in the Lord and in the power of His might. I can do all things, but not in myself. I can do all things through Christ Who strengthens me. I am great, but not in myself. I am great because the greater one lives in me. Rehearsing these will keep us humble, which is so important if we want God to lift us up. Remaining humble is our responsibility. No one can humble us. We can't even pray and ask God to humble us because that's not His job; but when we choose to humble ourselves, God will lift us up and exalt us.

James 4:10 Humble yourselves in the sight of the Lord, and he shall lift you up.

1 Peter 5:6 Humble yourselves therefore under the mighty hand of God, that he may exalt you in due time.

In ourselves, we may be nothing, know nothing, have nothing, and can do nothing, but we are no longer in ourselves. We are in Christ Jesus! These "In Christ" realities are good reminders of who we are and what we have in Him.

1. In Christ, I am loved, accepted, righteous (and so much more).
2. In Christ, I know all things (because I have the mind of Christ).
3. In Christ, I have all things (because your hand is open to every living thing).
4. In Christ, I can do all things (because the Lord strengthens me).

This is what being humble is all about because we know it's in Him that we are loved, know, have, and can do all things. When I read 1 Peter 5:6 about God exalting us when we humble ourselves under His mighty hand, it just popped off the page at me. It was so strong that it was as if God's hand had slapped me. Then He said to me, "You talk about My hand not being shortened. You talk about My hand being open, but there's something about My mighty hand that I want to show you, these people, and My church." During a time of prophecy, the Lord also said, "For in My grace shall you walk, in My grace shall you stand, and you will surely see My great and mighty hand." That prophecy was meant for everyone in the body of Christ.

So, when I took this utterance (You will surely see My great and mighty hand) and connected it to James 4:10 (Humble yourselves in the sight of the Lord, and He shall lift you up) and 1 Peter 5:6 (Humble yourself under God's mighty hand), it showed me that He is the one who is exalting and lifting us up with His mighty hand. So, when I visualize myself under His mighty hand, and I take my hands off of whatever I am going through, then He has it in is His hands, and He will lift me up. Are you ready to be lifted up? Then humble yourself under His mighty hand.

God taught me a very valuable lesson about who it is that lifts me up and exalts me. Once, when I was preaching, the Holy Ghost revealed to me the thoughts of someone in the congregation. I could hear this person saying to themselves, "Why is he up there? What makes him so special? I'm just as good a preacher as he is." What that person was thinking may have been factual, but no matter how much someone knows or how gifted they might be, it won't move God to get them in the pulpit. They could promote themselves into a pulpit, but their ability won't move God to put them there. With God, it all comes down to being humble before Him and submitting ourselves to Him, and I suspect the person's thoughts I heard that day hadn't done either. God put me in the office of pastor, not because of my talent or ability, but because I was submitted to Him. In myself, I know I can't do it, so I just obey His leadings and do what He says by the unction and strength of the Holy Ghost. Pride would say, "I've got this," but humility says, "Lord, you've got this, and I'm going to follow you." That means there may be times when we need to zip our lips and just trust God. It's not always easy, but we all can do it! I am so glad I don't have to figure things out on my own, and I can go to God who has all the answers.

In the King James version, the Bible says we are to clothe ourselves, with humility, and not to let anybody strip humility away from us. I like the way the Amplified Classic puts it.

> *1 Peter 5:5 (AMPC) ...Clothe (apron) yourselves, all of you, with humility [as the garb of a servant, so that its covering cannot possibly be stripped from you, with freedom from pride and arrogance] toward one another. For God sets Himself against the proud (the insolent, the overbearing, the disdainful, the presumptuous, the boastful) - [and He opposes, frustrates, and defeats them], but gives grace (favor, blessing) to the humble.*

When I clothe myself, with humility, like a garment, God's power can come on my life, like a garment.

> *James 4:7 <u>Submit yourselves therefore to God</u>. Resist the devil, and he will flee from you.*

James purposely wrote it this way because before we can stand in God's grace to resist the enemy and use our authority to make him flee, we must first be submitted to God. Believers like the last part of this scripture that says, "Resist the devil and he will flee," but they don't get as excited about the first part which says, "Submit yourselves to God."

To "submit" means to accept, or yield to God's way of doing things; "resist" means to stand against the works and temptations the devil brings to our flesh to get us to sin. When we're submitted to God, we won't fall into his trap, which is opposite of what the devil wants. Why is the enemy wanting to get us into sin? Because He knows we won't be able to walk in God's standing grace that will not only keep us free from sin but will also put us in position to help others get and stay free from the enemy's bondage too.

It's God's standing grace that we need to resist disappointment, depression, sickness, disease, or whatever the devil brings; in order to receive God's grace, we must humble ourselves under His mighty hand and submit to Him.

Some Christians who are not submitted to God and His Word think they can get the enemy to flee by just saying, "In Jesus' name," like it's some sort of lucky rabbit's foot; but no matter how many times they use His name, it won't work until they are truly submitted to God.

So many people blame everyone and everything around them when bad things happen, which is typical, and a worldly thing to do; for a believer, when something in our life isn't working, or the devil isn't fleeing, we should be asking ourselves, "Am I submitted to God?" Submitting is a choice, which means we can choose to submit, or we can choose not to submit.

How do we submit ourselves to God? By submitting to His Word, His voice, and to the elders God has placed over us. Let's look at each one of these in more detail.

1. Submit to God's Word

We can only submit to God's Word when we know what it says, so submitting to His Word means reading, and studying, and then applying it. James 1:22 says, "Be ye doers of the word, and not hearers only, deceiving your own selves." So, when a believer says they're submitted to God's Word, but they're not doing what the Word says, they have deceived themselves and will not be able to walk in God's standing grace. That's when the devil will be able run over them morning, noon, and night. We must submit to God's Word in every area of our lives if we want to walk in God's power and authority needed to have the abundant life God has ordained for us.

2. Submit to God's voice

Submitting to His voice means to follow His leadings,

and not just the ones we want to follow. Why would someone not follow God's leading? Because they don't want to do it, and since they would never say, "No," to God, they just pretend like they didn't hear Him. It's no different than children who are playing and pretending not to hear their parents, or a husband watching TV and pretending not to hear his wife. When it comes to God, we can all submit to His voice because once we are born again, we can hear His voice. We don't have to learn it because all believers know the voice of their Good Shepherd; acting like we can't or didn't hear it won't get anyone off the hook with God because He knows our thoughts.

For new believers, as well as other Christians, who say they can't hear His voice, a good place to start would be to tune their spiritual ears to His voice inwardly by meditating on the following scriptures and then confessing them often, so their faith will grow, and their spiritual ears will be opened to hearing His voice.

John 10:3-5

3 To him the porter openeth; and the sheep hear his voice: and he calleth his own sheep by name, and leadeth them out.

4 And when he putteth forth his own sheep, he goeth before them, and the sheep follow him: for they know his voice.

[5] And a stranger will they not follow, but will flee from him: for they know not the voice of strangers.

Confess: I am His sheep; I know His voice and the voice of stranger I will not follow.

John 18:37 ... Every one that is of the truth heareth my [Jesus'] voice.

Confess: I am of the truth, and I hear His voice.

John 16:13 Howbeit when he, the Spirit of truth, is come, he will guide you into all truth: for he shall not speak of himself; but whatsoever he shall hear, that shall he speak: and he will shew you things to come.

Confess: The Holy Spirit will guide me into all truth and will show me things to come.

Romans 8:14 For as many as are led by the Spirit of God, they are the sons of God.

Confess: Because I am His child, I am led by the Spirit of God.

John 2:20 But ye have an unction from the Holy One, and ye know all things.

Confess: I have an unction from the Holy Ghost,

and I know all things.

Revelation 2:7 He that hath an ear, let him hear what the Spirit saith unto the churches....

Confess: Because I am part of the church, I hear what the Spirit of God is saying to me.

The more Word we put in our heart, the more we will be able to hear God speak to us because He will only speak in line with His Word.

No one likes having to submit. I don't like it either, so how am I able to submit to the Lord? For the same reason my wife is able to submit to me. It's because she knows that I love her, and that I want the best for her; just like I know that God loves me and wants the best for me. Because I know this, it's not hard for me to submit to His voice.

3. <u>Submit to the elders God has placed over us</u>

1 Peter 5:5 (NKJV) Likewise you younger people, submit yourselves to your elders.

A lot of people think they're submitted to those God has placed over them, but agreement is not submission. It's only when we disagree, or they give us correction, or they ask us to do something in the church we don't want to do, that we really find out if we're submitted. We have to check ourselves on this, because if our flesh is resisting our elders, then we are not submitted.

Once, when I was ministering overseas, some of the pastors were complaining to me saying, "Nobody submits to me." Later, I responded quite loudly from the pulpit to all of them and said, "If someone is not submitting to you, maybe they don't think you love them." I said that by the Holy Ghost. I think God just wanted to wake them up because it's so important for them to understand that the more love they show to those under their authority, the easier it will be for them to submit to their leadership. Now, when it comes to us personally, we should submit to our leaders, whether we think they love us or not, because we know that's what the Word says.

> *Hebrews 13:17 Obey them that have the rule over you, and submit yourselves: for they watch for your souls, as they that must give account, that they may do it with joy, and not with grief: for that is unprofitable for you.*

Leaders who themselves won't receive what is being said or are not willing to do what is asked of them, are not really submitted to those who have been placed over them. No one can make someone submit to the person in authority over them. Even God won't make us submit. We each have to choose to submit to them, and we can, when we realize how much God loves us and is for us.

So, once we're submitted to His Word, His voice, and those in authority over us, we can receive and walk in this grace to stand against the enemy.

Standing against the enemy.

> *John 10:10 The thief, the devil, comes to steal,*
> *kill, and destroy…*

As Christians, we will encounter the enemy's works because the Word says that Satan is the god of this world, so he's not going away.

> *2 Corinthians 4:4 (NLT) Satan, who is the god*
> *of this world, has blinded the minds of those*
> *who don't believe. They are unable to see the*
> *glorious light of the Good News. They don't*
> *understand this message about the glory of*
> *Christ, who is the exact likeness of God.*

Even if the enemy leaves for a season, like he did after tempting Jesus in the wilderness, he will always return; but with this standing grace, we can resist him.

Part of standing against the enemy is seeing him the way Jesus sees him and that is as a defeated foe. Colossians 2:15 says that Jesus destroyed him, and made a show of him openly, triumphing over him in it. What is "in it"? It's Jesus' death, burial, resurrection, and ascension, so this scripture is telling us that the victory has already been won. Jesus has already redeemed us from sin, sickness, disease, poverty, and anything else that the enemy may try to bring. But even though the work of Jesus is finished, our part is to enforce this victory by standing against the enemy in God's standing grace; and when we do, the devil will flee, and we will walk in total and complete victory.

It doesn't matter what the devil brings against us, or the diagnosis given; we don't have to receive it because the Word of God is above it. The devil will always try to move us with bad reports, and by the things we see and hear, and how we feel, but we must believe the report of the Lord (Isaiah 53:1), so we will not be moved.

When someone is moved from their faith, it's because they have become double minded in their thinking. Being double minded is someone having two mindsets, believing the Word, but then believing what the world or circumstances around them say. The Bible says, when we waver in that way, we can't expect to receive anything from God.

James 1:6-8

⁶ But let him ask in faith, nothing wavering. For he that wavereth is like a wave of the sea driven with the wind and tossed.

⁷ For let not that man think that he shall receive any thing of the Lord.

[8] *A double minded man is unstable in all his ways*.

It says that a double minded man is unstable. We have to be of one mind by agreeing with the Word, so we can be stable and not be moved.

I can remember when I first came to Alabama to start the church. Since this was God's plan for me, I prepared for 100 people for my first service, but only one woman with her two daughters came. The next week, no one came. It was just me and the couple who had moved here with me to help start the church, so I sat them down and preached my sermon to them. It was one of the hardest things I have ever done. Later that day, I looked up to heaven and said, "God, where are you? What's up?" I was devastated. I felt so bad, that I couldn't eat, and anyone who knows me knows when I can't eat, it's a big deal. Then, someone I trusted called me and said, "Mark, you're called to the ministry, but it takes a special man to pioneer a church. Perhaps you're not that man." That sure kicked me while I was down. Others called saying, "Did you make a mistake?" I had left my family, my church, and my ministry with very little money to rent a store front building and got a job that barely paid my own rent, so moving back home became very tempting.

It came down to this. Would I let circumstances move me out of what I believed God's plan was for my life, or would I trust God and keep going? I had to decide, so I went home, got down on my knees and asked God, "Is this your will for me? Tell me right now if I'm in the right place, and I'll never ask you again." Before my nose hit the dirty brown carpet, God said, "You're doing the right thing, at the right time, in the right place." That was it for me. I immediately got up because I now had a Word from the Lord, a Rhema Cristos, that gave me the faith I needed to keep doing what God had called me to do.

So, with the standing grace given to me by this Rhema Word God had spoken to me, I was now moved by faith again. I still didn't have any money, but somehow the Lord took care of me. I rented the building by faith. I got the chairs by faith, and I got a sound system by faith. I just didn't have any people yet, but then God moved miraculously. The Sunday after I had talked to God, this woman walked through the door of the church, and when she did, the Holy Ghost said to me, "From this day forward, you'll never do anything but grow," and that's what has happened. How? Only God knows. My part was to stand in His grace and keep going.

The devil still tried to move me, but he couldn't because I had stepped into the grace to stand against his attack. If the enemy could have stopped me, the church that I pastor today would not be here. We cannot let the devil or circumstances keep us from what God has called us to do. In my case, the church didn't immediately grow, but I had the faith to stand until it did because I had heard from God. From that point on, when someone would say something, instead of pondering and wondering if they were right, I would remember what God had said knowing I was doing the right thing, which enabled me to stand and continue to walk in the will of God for my life.

We will all have opportunities to waver and be of two mindsets. Even Peter wavered when he walked on the water to Jesus. He started out in faith and did well, but then when circumstances (winds) came, it caused him to waver and become double minded. That's when he became unstable and started to sink; then Jesus came and set Peter standing on the water again. When anyone finds themselves wavering, they should take it back to God, so He can tell them again, and He will, just like He did with me. When we are walking on His Word and standing in His grace, we will only be moved by faith and not by circumstances.

There are pivotal moments in life when we have to choose whether we will listen to God, or everything and everybody around us. We have to decide if we will continue to stand or not. If I had not listened to God and stood in His grace, my whole life would have been different.

Colossians 1:23 If ye continue in the faith grounded and settled, and be not moved away from the hope of the gospel, which ye have

*heard, and which was preached to every
creature which is under heaven; whereof I Paul
am made a minister.*

If we don't listen to God and let Him lead us, the devil will try to lead us. And if we don't continue in faith, then we are allowing the devil to move us through circumstances and the people around us. We should only be moved by what God says and trust Him to work things out. If God isn't saying anything, then just keep doing the last thing He told you to do. God is a good communicator, so if anything needs to change, He will tell you. God is not withholding anything from us. He will lead and guide us in the way we should go when we listen.

Whenever I say, "Lord, I'm just really getting tired of this," I hear Him say on the inside, "Being tired is not a strategy." It reminds me that we can't grow weary or tired because this will cause us to be moved away from the Word of God. We just need His plan, His strategy.

Just remember, no matter what the devil is doing in the world, it doesn't have to come near us when we stand against it by God's grace. Now, I'm not saying we are to stand against people because we don't wrestle with flesh and blood (Ephesians 6:12), but we are to stand against what the enemy may try to do through people. And when we stand against the devil, the thief, and resist, we will win every battle and experience the abundant life the Lord has provided for us.

*John 10:10 [Jesus said] The thief cometh not,
but for to steal, and to kill, and to destroy: I am
come that they might have life, and that they
might have it more abundantly.*

If things seem messed up and someone says, "Where's God?" I'll tell them where He is. He's sitting on the throne. He's living in us. And what is He doing? He's waiting on us to believe His Word and then do it. We're not waiting on God; He's waiting on us. So, when the devil comes with his temptations of sickness, poverty, confusion, circumstances, or whatever it is, we can resist him standing in this grace because we know Jesus will give us the victory He has already won if we will keep standing. If you find yourself needing more grace to stand, go back to the throne room and receive the more that you need. That's what I do. I submit and humble myself under God's mighty hand, and then, I believe that I now have the standing grace I need to walk out whatever I'm facing. I know that the one, I serve has defeated him. I know that Jesus lives in me. I know I have the name of Jesus, which is above every other name. And I know I can access, by faith, standing grace, His ability, to resist and stand against the enemy.

When stuff starts happening in our lives, and we seem bothered on every side, we should spend more time in the throne room to obtain more mercy and find more grace in our time of need. We can also help others by taking them to the throne room to receive the mercy and grace they need. So, if you're having trouble resisting the devil, spend more time in God's Word and in prayer, so you can stand against the wiles of the devil. Spending more time in His Word and in His presence is always the answer.

One of the tactics the devil will use is to tell you, "You're a special case." What is he doing? He's trying to convince you that your case is too difficult, or too hard for God, but that's a lie. No one is so special that the Word and His grace won't work for them, but it will only work for those who are doing the Word and obeying His leadings. It's okay to do things in the natural, like going to the doctor, seeking wise counsel, and so on, as long as we don't trust, rely, or lean on them above God's Word. God and His Word must always be first place because when we do it God's way, we will see the victory.

I remember, when I was going into a new season in my church, someone said to me, "You know, with this new level, come bigger devils." I thought, "I don't like the devils I'm dealing with now, so I don't know if I want to start a new season." It shook my confidence just a bit but thank God for strong believers in the Lord around us. This sweet lady in our church, who sensed what was happening, came to me and said, "Pastor Mark, the devils, no matter how big they get, they are still under your feet." That helped me so much to steady myself again. We all need help like that from time to time.

So, it doesn't matter what the enemy brings, God's standing grace is more than enough to put the enemy in his place. I remember some years back, when I was going through something, I got to the place where I had just had it. I felt like the weight of it was just too much for me to go on, that it was too hard, and it would just be easier for me to give up; then I remembered Paul. I felt like if I came face to face with Paul right then, he would say to me, "Toughen up, buttercup." Why? Because Paul had gone through so much more than I could ever imagine. Paul, one of the major apostles, had seen the Lord and was given so much revelation that he, by the Holy Ghost, wrote two-thirds of the New Testament and had also faced more problems than most. Everywhere Paul went, people were trying to kill him. Paul was beaten, stoned, shipwrecked, and imprisoned. Paul finally sought the Lord's help because he was reaching his breaking point.

2 Corinthians 12:8 (NKJV) <u>Concerning this thing</u> I pleaded with the Lord three times that it might depart from me.

I can just imagine that when Paul called upon the Lord for help in this matter, that the Lord was thinking, "Finally, we can talk about this." Why? Because God is always waiting for us to come to Him, so He can show us what to do. What was this "it" that Paul was referring to? Paul called the "it" a "thorn in the flesh," but Paul also said that "it" was a messenger of Satan (2 Corinthians 12:8). It was a demon that was continually messing with him to trip him up; Paul asked the Lord to get rid of it, but instead of removing it, the Lord said,

> *2 Corinthians 12:9 (NKJV) ... <u>My grace is sufficient for you</u>, for My strength is made perfect in weakness.*

This scripture is talking about standing grace. You could say it like this, "My standing grace is sufficient for you."

Many believers misinterpret, "My grace is sufficient," and think the Lord is saying, "Just hang on," or "Endure it," but what He is actually saying is that His grace is more than enough to resist whatever comes. In the Greek, "sufficient" means to be enough to meet your needs, to ward off, or be a barrier against. In other words, God's grace was all that Paul needed to ward off and stand against any demon and get rid of it, but this is only true for those who are submitted to God.

A lot of people, instead of standing in God's "sufficient" grace, just want God to fix it and will pray, "Lord, do something about my sickness," "Lord, do something about my lack," "Lord, do something about my life," "Lord, do something!" When we really listen to the Lord's reply, He will say the same thing to us that He said to Paul, "My grace is sufficient." What does that mean? God is saying, "I've already fixed it. It's done. So, receive my grace; walk in it, and My grace will take care of this."

Because this conversation between Paul and God was after the resurrection of Jesus, Paul already had the revelation that believers were raised up and seated with Jesus far above all principalities, power, might and dominion (Ephesians 1:20-21); so, when the Lord said His grace was sufficient, Paul didn't think, "Oh, no!" or "Oh my!" Instead, he realized that this was his opportunity to walk in the standing power of God.

A lot of people think, "Well, if you really had faith, you'd never have any problems." I don't know where believers got the idea that the devil will never bother them once they're born again. The truth is, we don't know if we have faith until we've got a problem to deal with.

Years back, someone asked my spiritual father to, "Pray that the devil will leave me alone," but he knew he couldn't pray that. He said that to pray for the enemy to leave someone alone, he would have to pray for the Lord to kill them because as long as we live on the earth, and the enemy is the god of this world, he is not going to leave us alone. What we must do is to step into God's grace because that's what we need in order to stand firm and win against whatever the enemy is doing or brings our way. When we resist him in this grace, we will have

God's eternal weight of glory come upon us. And when we have the revelation that God's grace is sufficient for us, we, like Paul, can say, "When I am weak, I'm really strong, not in my own strength, but I am strong in the power of God. Amen." Paul understood this and was able to receive God's all sufficient grace needed to stand against what the enemy was doing and was able to say...

2 Corinthians 12:9-10 (NKJV)

[9] ... Therefore most gladly I will rather boast in my infirmities, that the power of Christ may rest upon me.

[10] Therefore I take pleasure in infirmities, in reproaches, in needs, in persecutions, in distresses, for Christ's sake. For when I am weak, then I am strong.

Paul knew he was no match for the devil, and that his strength was only made perfect by God's grace, His power. Why didn't the Lord just say, "I'll take care of it?" Because He already had! That's like saying, "Lord, heal me," or "Lord, save me," when the Bible says He's already done both, and so much more! It's a finished work, so Jesus doesn't need to go to the cross every time we have a need or a problem. He has already taken care of it for us by providing everything we need for life and godliness, so we can take care of it in His authority and power. It's now up to us to respond to the leadings of the Holy Ghost and do what the Bible says.

From the verses we've read, we can see that it's God's strength, His grace to stand in, that we need; if we don't have His grace, we won't be able to stand against what the devil is doing. It's like we're in a circle of grace. When we humble and submit ourselves to God, we're standing in the center of this circle; but when we get into pride or disobedience, we step out of this circle of grace, where we are no match for the enemy.

When some believers hear, "My grace is sufficient for you," they will say, "Well, the Lord will never give you more than you can bear." That's not right, and it's not scriptural. They are misquoting 1 Corinthians 10:13.

> *1 Corinthians 10:13 There hath no temptation taken you but such as is common to man: but God is faithful, who will not suffer you to be tempted above that ye are able; but will with the temptation <u>also make a way to escape</u>, that ye may be able to bear it.*

What this verse is actually saying, is God will always make a way of escape, so we will be able to bear it. The Lord has never given us anything bad, but when bad things come, He will give us an escape route. With standing grace, we can get out of everything the enemy throws at us. That's why I can willingly submit everything to God because I know when I humble myself under His mighty hand, He's going to pick me up. So, when the devil comes, I know, because I am standing in

His circle of grace, I can resist any attack of the enemy, and so can you!

We must also remain on guard, so when the enemy does come, we can be quick to run him off.

1 Peter 5:8-10 (NKJV)

[8] Be sober, be vigilant; because your adversary the devil walks about like a roaring lion, seeking whom he may devour.

[9] Resist him, steadfast in the faith, knowing that the same sufferings [afflictions] are experienced by your brotherhood in the world.

[10] But the God of all grace, who hath called us unto his eternal glory by Christ Jesus, <u>after that ye have suffered a while</u>, make you perfect, stablish, strengthen, settle you.

It says, "after you have suffered." Suffer? Yes. I looked it up in other translations and it still says suffer. "Suffer" just means to be subject to something bad or unpleasant; but thank God, it says "after you have suffered a while," so it doesn't have to be for long and it's definitely not supposed to be forever. Suffering does come, so it's silly to ignore it or pretend it doesn't exist. That kind of thinking will get us in a ditch. The other side of the ditch are those who do not ignore it, but then act like the devil is so big and mighty that they have to run scared of him. Both ditches will get you in trouble.

Know that Jesus understands our suffering. He is our high priest and will keep us. Suffering comes to every believer, but God has provided the grace to get rid of whatever it is. Just don't become so conscious of the devil that it seems like you're glorifying him. Don't become a suffering saint who is always telling those around them everything that's going on. When we complain, talk about, or give reverence to what the devil is doing, it's like saying, "sic 'em," to a dog. This is opening the door wider for the enemy to bring more. What am I saying? When the enemy comes, stand against him by grace and tell him to go, in Jesus' name, and then go on with your day, but you can only do this if you have humbled yourself and submitted yourself to God.

What else can we do when the enemy comes? We can rejoice because this is an opportunity for us to stand against him, use our authority, and see the victory that the Lord will bring. We also need to be saying what the Word has to say about it because we have a name that's above whatever is happening. That's how we overcome, by the blood of the Lamb and the word of our testimony; the word "overcome" is present tense. The devil exists, but nothing is too big for God, so exercise your authority and chase him off. God will always cause you to triumph when you fight the good fight of faith, and a good fight is one you win! We will always come out of it on the winning side when we stand in His grace, and each time we do, we will get stronger.

It's like going to the gym and lifting weights. When we lift weights, we are building muscle, but if we don't resist the weight, it could crush us. It's the same when the devil comes to kill, steal, or destroy. If we don't resist what he's bringing, it could crush us; but when we do resist, we are building our faith muscles. So, when the enemy comes against me, I'm going to resist him in God's standing grace, in the name of Jesus, and I'm going to command him to go. What am I doing? I'm using the authority God has given me to make the devil flee. Every time I do, my faith muscles are getting bigger, and I'm being established, strengthened, and settled.

We need to build our faith muscles, and that can only be done when we understand His grace. Grace and faith always work together. God is saying, "Here's My power (grace) to stand." So that means when the enemy comes, you can, by faith, resist him. We must realize that we can't stand by our own power or might. It can only be done by His Spirit (Zechariah 4:6), the Spirit of Grace, the Spirit of Power, the same Holy Spirit, who raised Jesus Christ from the dead and has raised us up with Him. Let's receive this grace, so we can stand!

Paul continued to receive more revelation of standing grace and said in Ephesians 6, "After you've done all to stand, stand, therefore." Those who fight wear armor.

We, too, have armor. It is the armor of God that we are supposed to put on, and once we do, we should never take it off. This armor is our protection and weapon to withstand the attacks of the enemy.

Ephesians 6:10-18

[10] Finally, my brethren, be strong in the Lord,
and in the power of his might.

[11] <u>Put on the whole armour of God, that ye may</u>
<u>be able to stand against the wiles of the devil</u>.

[12] For we wrestle not against flesh and blood,
but against principalities, against powers,
against the rulers of the darkness of this world,
against spiritual wickedness in high places.

[13] Wherefore take unto you the whole armour of
God, that ye may be able to withstand in the evil
day, and <u>having done all, to stand.</u>

[14] <u>Stand therefore</u>, having your <u>loins girt about</u>
<u>with truth</u>, and having on the <u>breastplate of</u>
<u>righteousness</u>.

[15] And your <u>feet shod with the preparation of the</u>
<u>gospel of peace</u>;

[16] Above all, taking the <u>shield of faith</u>,
wherewith ye shall be able to quench all the
fiery darts of the wicked.

[17] And take the <u>helmet of salvation</u>, and the

sword of the Spirit, which is the word of God:

¹⁸ *Praying always with all prayer and supplication in the Spirit, and watching thereunto with all perseverance and supplication for all saints.*

We are told in Verse 10, "Be strong in the Lord." We do that by wearing our armor and using our sword, which is speaking the Word of God. That's how we stand in His grace. God has shown me that I must see myself standing in His power, in His ability; not in my own strength, but in His supernatural grace; and when I do, I can resist any affliction, persecution, or whatever the devil tries to bring.

Ephesians 6:18 said to pray always, so whenever I feel like the devil is winning, or I can't seem to get out of a situation, I know it's because I lack understanding on this. When that happens, I always pray, "Lord, open my eyes, so I can see all that grace is, and all you have provided, so I can stand; and having done all to stand, I can continue to stand."

To be able to stand in His grace, it's also important to cast <u>all</u> of our cares upon the Lord.

Psalm 55:22 Cast thy burden upon the Lord, and he shall sustain thee: he shall never suffer the righteous to be moved.

Why is it so important to do this? Because when cares, problems, and burdens come, they're all we think about, which can cause us to get off track by making us doubt and wonder. This will cause us to be double minded. So, instead of taking cares and keeping them, we should always give them to God by casting them on Him, so we can then get back to what God has told us to do.

How can believers resist the enemy and win?

- Humble yourself under God's mighty hand.
- Submit yourself to God.
- Receive standing grace to resist the enemy and his works.
- Resist the enemy.
- Wear your armor and use your weapon.
- Pray always.
- Walk in His Spirit and not in your own might or power.
- Don't be moved from the Word of God.
- Cast all your cares upon the Lord.

This is our playbook to stand against the enemy, and when we follow it, we will win every time.

Chapter 05

SERVING GRACE

Serving grace is the empowerment that has been made available to every born-again believer to serve others in the church and to fulfill what God has called them to do in life.

> *2 Timothy 1:9 Who hath saved us, and <u>called us</u> <u>with an holy calling</u>, not according to our works, but according <u>to his own purpose and</u> <u>grace</u>, which was given us in Christ Jesus before the world began.*

God has a purpose, a plan, a destiny for everyone on the planet, but it starts with being born again. When you were in your mother's womb, the Lord knew you (Jeremiah 1:5); and before you did anything right or wrong, He called you to His purpose and gave you grace to enable you to accomplish this calling, which is stamped on the inside of you, like a blueprint. Faith and prayer will bring it forth and His grace will fulfill it. If we're not doing what God has called us to do, then there is no serving grace for us to access. I've been doing this for a long time, and what I've found is that if I don't tap into God's serving grace, it will affect my entire walk.

The Lord has a purpose for each one of us. That purpose is not our decision, but our discovery. Fulfilling our purpose reminds me of an exercise bike I used to have. The bike's intended purpose was for me to get on it and exercise, but instead, I would use it as a clothes rack. I could hang several shirts and lay my slacks over the handlebars, and even put my shoes on the seat. It was a great clothes rack, but that was not its intended or highest purpose. We don't want to be like that exercise bike. Let's find out what God has called us to do and then do it.

Discovering our purpose is so important. That's why we shouldn't tell our children, "Baby, you can be whatever you want to be." That sounds good, but that's not allowing them to achieve the highest purpose that God has for them. What parents should say to their children is, "Baby, you can be whatever God wants you to be, and I will do all I can to help you discover your purpose in life." Making that adjustment will help your child reach for everything God has ordained them to be. As a parent, we should take them like an arrow and aim them towards God to discover their calling, so they can obtain their healthiest, happiest, and most fulfilled life.

We should all want to find God's intended purpose for our life. One of the best ways I know to do that is to serve one another at church. Whatever your passion might be or however God is leading you, serve in that area, and it will lead you to the place God has for you. We have all been given this ability to serve, so we need to get to it.

> *1 Peter 4:10 As every man hath received the*
> *gift, even so minister the same one to another,*
> *as good stewards of the <u>manifold grace of God</u>.*

This grace to serve has been made available to us as a gift, which means we can't earn it. Our part is to receive this grace, by faith, because everyone in the body of Christ is called to serve. The Bible likens the body of Christ to our physical body.

> *1 Corinthians 12:12 For as the body is one, and*
> *hath many members, and all the members of*
> *that one body, being many, are one body: so*
> *also is [the body of] Christ.*

Our physical body has many parts, hands, arms, legs, feet, eyes, lungs, and so on. If certain parts are missing, our physical body can still function, but it's so much better when all our parts are working because that's when we are the strongest and functioning at our highest; the same is true for the body of Christ. Ephesians 4:16 says that the whole body is fitly joined together with every joint supplying. I like the way the New Living Translation puts it.

> *Ephesians 4:16 (NLT) He makes the whole body fit together perfectly. As each part does its own special work, it helps the other parts grow, so that the whole body is healthy and growing and full of love.*

We need every part working (serving) in order to have a healthy body. Every person has something to do for God, and 1 Corinthians 12 says that the parts less seen are due even more honor than the parts that are seen. What does that mean? It's talking about the people who do so many vital things in the church but are not seen like those who are out front ministering and leading. To them, who are not seen, God bestows more honor.

Many Christians think that serving is only meant for those called to the ministry, but that's just wrong thinking. Those in the ministry only make up about 5%, so what about the other 95% of the body of Christ? Does God intend for them to just sit on the sidelines and do nothing? Absolutely not. Everyone in the body of Christ is called to serve. So many in the churches of today don't seem to understand that, and are going back to wanting to be served, but that's not how God set it up. We are all to serve, love, and pray for one another. Everyone in the body of Christ has been given an assignment and serving grace they can access by faith to complete their assignment. If someone thinks that God's plan for them is not very important, or nothing special, then I would say, they either haven't gotten to their plan yet, or they are not esteeming the place they are in, because everybody's plan, every place of service is important to the body of Christ. That's why receiving teaching on this is so important because we want every believer to find their place and understand how to receive the serving grace God has for them. We should be encouraging those not serving that they too have something to do for God.

For anyone who says, "I don't have time to serve," they just need to rearrange their schedule, because everyone should find time to serve. I'm sure glad Jesus found the time to go to the cross for us. If we want to get to our plan and do big things for God, it starts with serving somewhere. My spiritual father used to say, "God can't steer a parked bus." Be who God has called you to be, and until you find that place, just help somewhere in the church, so God can steer you to where you're supposed to be.

Serving one another is the mark of a Christian that says we love and prefer one another. It is our corresponding action.

*Romans 12:10 Be kindly affectioned one to
another with brotherly love; in honour
preferring one another.*

When we show the love of God to others, it will keep us
from focusing on ourselves so much. Just ask the Lord,
"How can I serve somebody?" Serving one another is a
sign and a wonder in these last days, to show the world
that we believe in taking care of each other.

We can all serve by finding ways to be kind, especially
to those who have not been kind to us. And, instead of
wanting somebody to get what's coming to them, why
don't we just be kind to them, so they can experience the
love of God? Even the people who have done us the
dirtiest, let's do what the Bible says and forgive them;
when they need comforting, let's comfort them; when
they need edifying, let's edify them; and when they need
strengthening, let's pray for them. When we serve
others, it will mess with them in a good way and soften
their hearts to receive the love of God. I'm not saying
you have to be their best buddy, but what I am saying is
that we must have a servant's heart to those around us.
It's not always easy, but it's what we are called to do, so
that means we can do it!

There are so many benefits to serving because this same
serving grace that enables us to serve in the church will
also help us in what we're called to do during the week.
The mistake I've seen many Christians make is that they

tap into their grace when they serve at church but then, don't know how to tap into it in their daily life, and they end up living two separate lives, a sacred life at church and a secular life during the week. God has given us only one life, and this serving grace is meant to enable us in all we do, both at church and outside the church. When you learn how to cooperate with this grace, it will abound for you during the week. This grace will bring promotions, bonuses, and raises. How? His grace brings favor. Psalm 5:12 says, "Favor surrounds you like a shield."

> *1 Corinthians 15:10 But by the grace of God I am what I am: and his grace which was bestowed upon me was not in vain; but I laboured more abundantly than they all: yet not I, but the grace of God which was with me.*

This is talking about who God has called us to be, and how His grace, freely bestowed on us, will enable us to labor even more abundantly in our serving.

Some people have twisted this verse to say, "Well, I am what I am, so that means God made me this way and that's why I act the way I do." God has definitely made each one of us to be who we are, but He didn't make anyone to act in a wrong way. Everyone has been given the freedom of choice, so it's up to us to choose how we will act. Be careful of anyone who wrests the scripture in this way and says, "It's okay for me to sin because

God made me this way." They're just trying to justify their wrong behavior. We live in a fallen world, and we all have wrong fleshly desires that must be put under; we also have an enemy that wants us to sin. That's why it's important to remain diligent and make right choices, so we don't fall into sin. God hasn't made anyone to sin and would never have anyone do anything that opposes His Word.

> *Galatians 5:13 For, brethren, ye have been called unto liberty; only use not liberty for an occasion to the flesh, but by love serve one another.*

This says that some Christians have misused the liberty God has given them as an excuse to sin, but God doesn't excuse sin, nor will He ever tempt anybody to sin.

> *James 1:13 Let no man say when he is tempted, I am tempted of God: for God cannot be tempted with evil, neither tempteth he any man.*

So, if God doesn't cause people to sin, who does? We do. We either choose to sin, or we're just not strong enough to resist it, so we fall into sin. For unbelievers, it's their nature. Dogs bark, fish swim, birds fly, cats meow, and sinners (unbelievers) sin because it's their nature. Because unbelievers are living out of their old nature, their flesh tends to dominate, which can cause them to live in and practice sin. That should not be so with believers, because when we were born again, we received a new nature; and when we walk in our new nature, we will not fall into sin.

Believers who habitually sin have overridden their new nature and given into temptation. This can happen, especially for those who are casual Christians, or those who haven't stayed in and obeyed the Word of God. We can all fall into sin. The good news is that God has given us 1 John 1:9, which says, "If we confess our sins, he is faithful and just to forgive us our sins, and to cleanse us from all unrighteousness." That doesn't mean it's okay to intentionally sin, but when we do fall into sin, we can get out of it by asking God to forgive us, so we can get right back to walking in our new nature again. Our new nature doesn't want to sin, so instead of letting our flesh do whatever it wants, we need to act out of our new nature and do what is right, as we continually strengthen and build our faith.

"I am what I am," is about who God has called you to be and what He has called you to do. Everybody has a place God has called them to, something they can put their hands to in order to help, and when they step into that place, they will find their grace.

Everyone who serves in the church, whether it's in the parking lot, as an usher, children's worker, nursery worker, greeter, cleaning team, or wherever it is, they can access the grace needed to do it. And this same grace that enables each one of us to serve in the church will also enable us to serve during our week, whether that's in the ministry, or as an accountant, engineer, teacher, lawyer, mechanic, someone running a household, someone raising children, or in whatever we do.

There are graces that God has ordained specifically for you concerning your career, business, and family, so it's not just about serving in the church, although that is an important part of it. I think all parents would agree, you need grace to raise children. Those who are married definitely need grace with their spouse. Those who are students need grace at school. Those who have a business, a career, or a job, need grace. We all need this grace to operate in, so we can achieve God's highest and best. Discover your place and embrace your grace; and when you do, you will find that there's so much more that God has waiting for you.

If you feel frustrated, you are probably trying to do things in your own strength. We are not sufficient in ourselves to do what He's called us to do, but His grace in us is sufficient, and more than enough, to do it but only when we choose to walk in it. By His grace, God can do so much more than we could ever do on our own, so let's walk in, live in, and minister by the grace of God. When you do, you won't get weary or become frustrated.

We all have a calling on our life, and we can't ignore it because we're afraid God might call us to do something we don't want to do, like pastoring or being a missionary in a foreign country. I'm not saying that couldn't happen, but so few are called to do that. What I am saying is that when we trust God and walk in the plan He has for our life, it will fulfill us, spirit, soul, and body. If we don't walk in serving grace because we choose not to serve, then the grace we need at work, in our business, in our home, and in our daily life won't be there either. Let's do what we need to do in order to access His serving grace!

When someone fights against or resists the calling God has for them, it will cause them to become very dissatisfied. Why? Because they are not fulfilling the will of God for their life. If anyone is feeling this way, just repent and let the Lord help you get into your place. He is a master at repositioning us. When we discover where we're supposed to be and what we're supposed to be doing and embrace it, the happier we will be, because we can now access serving grace, by faith, to empower us to do it and live the life God has ordained for us.

It's also important that we don't try to do something we're not called to do. If someone decides on their own that it would be great to start their own business or ministry, they will find it very difficult if God hasn't graced them to do it. I know it sounds great to be the one in charge, but the downside is that those in charge end up working long hours, with no sick days; and their vacation can get cut short if a problem comes up that they have to deal with. Someone employed doesn't have to deal with any of that. It takes grace to do whatever God has called us to do, so if God hasn't told you to start your own business, then it would be foolish to try. Just do what God has called you to do and fulfill His plan for your life. That is true success.

When we're in the right place, tapping into our grace, we won't want to trade what we're doing with anybody. I'm in my place and I love it! I'm happy, content, and fulfilled because I'm doing what God has called me to do. I'm so grateful for what God has given me. That's not to say there haven't been challenges and hard times along the way, but I know with God's grace, they are always doable.

When you get into the place God has for you, do it with all your heart unto Him (Colossians 3:23), knowing He is the one who has put you there.

1 Corinthians 1:26-27

26 For ye see your calling, brethren, how that not many wise men after the flesh, not many mighty, not many noble, are called:

27 But God hath chosen the foolish things of the world to confound the wise; and God hath chosen the weak things of the world to confound the things which are mighty.

This is a good scripture to remind us that we didn't call ourselves, but it was God who called us. It had nothing to do with anything we did, but everything to do with what He did. Our part was to obey and follow Him, because what He's called us to do isn't something we can do on our own anyway. I wouldn't even want to try pastoring without Him. We are all called to do great and mighty things for God, but this scripture will remind us not to get too big for our britches, because it's by His grace, and not by our works, that we are able to walk in the plan He has ordained for us. As we continue to do all that we do through Him, He will lead and guide us in the way we should go.

God spoke these words during a church service, and they apply to us all, "For in my grace you shall walk, and in my grace you shall stand." This is a good reminder that only when we stand in His grace can we do what He has called us to do. My wife and I follow those words and, on purpose, receive, by faith, His grace to pastor, and we teach our staff to do the same. Pastor Rhonda even teaches those who are on staff at the church to believe for "Pastor Mark and Pastor Rhonda" grace. We all need this serving grace, His enablement in every area of our lives to do what He has called us to do.

There are various kinds of grace to serve and to do and that's why it's so important who is appointed to a position, especially leadership. For example, we should not appoint someone as a praise and worship leader just because of their natural talent. We should appoint someone who has been graced to do it. If they are graced, the anointing will come but if they are not graced, it doesn't matter how great a singer they are, they're just singing songs. I would rather have someone graced and anointed in that position than someone who is a professional singer because only the grace will bring the anointing. We should always make sure that everyone appointed is graced to do it. Now, I will say that there are times, especially when a church is just beginning, that someone may be put in a position to fill a need and God will help them to do it, but they should only be considered temporary, as we believe God to bring in the person who has been graced to do it.

My wife and I can usually recognize when God has given a certain grace to someone. We have picked the pastoral staff and leaders that way because we saw the calling of God on their life and what they had been graced to do. It's also obvious to us when the grace isn't on someone to do certain things, and then it becomes our job to help them find their place by teaching them what the Word says.

To those who are currently serving but you feel like you don't want to do it anymore, that doesn't necessarily mean you're not in your place. It could mean you've let go of your grace and are trying to do it in your own strength. The fix for that is to make a heart adjustment and start confessing, "I've got the grace to do this." And for those who are doing something in the church or in their life, and God hasn't told them to stop or start something else, then they should just keep doing it and believe God for more grace.

This serving grace will make such a difference in your daily life. I've watched so many who serve in the church go higher, because they have taken their serving grace and let it flow into every part of their life. One of the biggest mistakes I've seen people make, is when things in their life start getting a little rough or they get busy, the first thing they do is pull away from serving in the church. By doing that, they have pulled away from their grace, and without this grace working in their life, things tend to become even more difficult. When someone stops serving, it's like they're saying to God, "No thanks, I don't need your grace at church anymore because I don't want to serve right now," but then, when they need this grace during their week, it's no longer there because they rejected it by not obeying God and serving in the church. If we want to live in a higher realm and walk in God's perfect will for our life, we need to understand our purpose, access and hold on to this grace to serve, and then finally, serve with all our heart unto the Lord.

God's grace can also move us from one assignment to another. I've had people say to me through the years, that they were doing a particular thing, but knew in their heart they were called to do something else. I remember this one man, who was part of the church early on; he was working in the family business but knew in his heart he was supposed to be a nurse. He finally quit the family business, went to school, became a nurse, and was the happiest he had ever been, because he was walking in his grace and now fulfilling his calling.

Grace is always there to enable us to do the good works God has called us to do (Ephesians 2:10). Serving grace is of the spirit, but it will also help us to do natural things with excellence, so access it and let it flow into every part of your life.

God's prearranged, preordained plan for each one of us is more than salvation, or the baptism of the Holy Spirit, or the gifts of the Spirit. It's about what He has specifically called us to do in the kingdom of God; and to get there, we must access the grace He has provided for us. How much grace we walk in is up to us, based on the amount we access. We can choose to access it all and continually receive more, or we can settle for just enough to do what we are doing today. I want to encourage everyone not to settle for just enough, or less than God's best. This grace was purchased for us at a high price, so let's access all of it and see where God wants to take us!

People are always asking me, "What is my purpose in life?" The best way for them to find out is to put their hands to something, so God can lead them to their place. Start serving; then, by faith, receive His grace needed to do it. When you do, you'll be amazed at how much fun it will be to serve, because God has wired us with a servant's heart. Just receive His serving grace, so you can run your race every day, Sunday through Saturday.

The Apostle Paul understood this and received serving grace to run His race.

Galatians 1:15-16

15 But when it pleased God, who separated me from my mother's womb, and called me by his grace,

16 To reveal his Son in me, that I might preach him among the heathen; immediately I conferred not with flesh and blood.

It pleased God to give Paul this grace to serve while he was still in his mother's womb, so that when Paul discovered his calling, he could access this grace to walk out the plan God had for him.

Ephesians 2:10 (AMPC) For we are God's [own] handiwork (His workmanship), recreated in Christ Jesus, [born anew] that we may do those good works which God predestined (planned beforehand) for us [taking paths which He prepared ahead of time], that we should walk in them [living the good life which He prearranged and made ready for us to live].

If someone is not living their good life, it's not because God's grace hasn't offered it. It's because this person hasn't learned how to receive the grace needed to walk it out. God has called us by His grace and predestined us all for good works, just like He did with Paul, and others in the Old Testament to include Joseph, Noah, and the prophets of old, and so many more. This grace (favor) was on their life in the same way that grace was on Paul's life, and this grace caused each one of them to do something in the kingdom of God. This grace on our lives will also cause us to do something, whether it's being in the ministry or doing something else. We all have our part to do in the body of Christ.

God has ordained for you so many wonderful things, and I'm so glad it's not based on our works or where we come from; it's according to His purpose and grace, and that, before the world began, He called us. What He offers is His best, His highest, the most fun, and the greatest life for you. Obtain the grace He has for you to walk in and find your place!

God's call on Paul's life was specific. He was given a specific grace to minister to the Gentiles. Grace can be that specific, or it can be more general, like someone called to own a business, or work at a particular company, or be in the "helps" ministry; then that grace can lead you to more.

Paul ministered to the Gentiles, but then God called him

to do more.

> *Romans 1:5 By whom we have received grace*
> *and apostleship, for obedience to the faith*
> *among all nations, for his name.*

Paul received more grace that enabled him not only to be a minister to the Gentiles, but to now be an apostle too. Paul didn't decide this. It was God's purpose for him. Paul had found his place and was then promoted to a new place and received the serving grace he needed to do it.

> *1 Corinthians 3:10 According to the grace of*
> *God which is given unto me, as a wise*
> *masterbuilder, I have laid the foundation, and*
> *another buildeth thereon. But let every man take*
> *heed how he buildeth thereupon.*

Paul's grace, given to him for his calling, made him a master builder in laying out the foundation that others would build on.

In the natural, even people who are outside the will of God or are not yet born again, still operate in a measure of grace, because, in their mother's womb, God has given them, as he has given to us all, talents and abilities. We all know people around us who are just naturally good at this or that; and it's because God has graced them with that ability, a grace that has always been there since birth. For me, I was always good at math, so when I graduated from college, I became an accountant. I've always enjoyed working with numbers, balance sheets, income statements, and graph charts, and still do; but this natural ability God gave me was not His call for my life. I was called to pastor, but in pastoring, I have used this natural ability in math to help me manage the finances of the church.

Whatever God gives us is never wasted. Somehow, it just all seems to fit together. These natural abilities are good to have, but it's still His serving grace we must fully walk in to do what He has call us to do, because that is what will truly enable us. When we access and walk in our serving grace each day, we will see good things start to happen in our lives.

Are you walking in His grace, or in your own strength? It's easy to tell the difference. We know when we're doing it on our own, or when God is doing it through us. Doing it on our own is labor, but when we let His serving grace empower us, it's a labor of love. Let this grace work in your life each day and watch things change.

Again, receiving all the grace He has for us is up to us.

Romans 12:6 Having then <u>gifts differing</u> <u>according to the grace that is given to us</u>, whether prophecy, let us prophesy <u>according to the proportion of faith</u>.

It's according to the amount (proportion) of faith we have that will determine how much grace we can receive. The grace on my life has always been there, from my mother's womb, but my ability to access it required me to grow in faith, and the more I did, the more grace I was able to access. So, grow in faith, and you, too, can grow in grace! Let's grow in every area of our lives. Let's grow in our understanding of what our salvation includes, so we can walk in more of His saving grace. Let's grow in living grace, so we can walk in victory. Let's grow in standing grace, so we can stand against the enemy. Let's grow in serving grace, so we can be all God has called us to be. And let's grow in grace to be rich (next chapter), so we can be well supplied.

We all have different graces and giftings. God has called each of us to be unique, and not to copy or act like somebody else. It's okay to imitate or find godly examples to show us how to do certain things or how to begin something, but we are not to try and be them. Let's be who God made us to be. Twins are a good example of this. To those around them, they may look alike, but they are not the same. Most people may not be able to tell them apart, but when you get to know them, you can see that they are very different and unique.

Graces are similar, but with differences too. We have a number of real estate agents in our church that are graced to do it, but their way of doing it is not the same. Their styles may be similar, but how they sell and work with their clients is different.   This is because of their uniqueness as an individual, and the grace they have received based on their faith.

The Apostle Paul was able to prophesy, minister, govern, teach, and be blessed based on the grace he accessed and received in proportion to what he believed.   When our faith increases, our grace will increase too, which means what we can receive from God will increase.   The only way to grow in faith is by hearing and doing the Word of God.   So, let's get in the Word and grow our faith to access more of the grace God has for us.   Then, let's keep growing our faith, so we can keep accessing even more grace.   When we believe for it and access His grace, by faith, we will find it.

I was a good accountant, but when I started accessing God's grace to serve, I became a great accountant. Whenever I had a problem I couldn't solve, I would go home that evening and pray about it, and the next day I would know what to do.   When I worked at McDonald's while going to Bible school, I became a great manager, because I accessed the serving grace that was on my life. McDonald's was so pleased with the job I did that they wanted to send me to Hamburger University (yes, there is such a place).   It wasn't me doing it, but the grace I walked in; God even used my job at McDonald's to train me for the ministry.   When I worked at the clothing store as a salesman, I sold very little, until God gave me a strategy.   He told me that instead of trying to sell, just help those who came in. His grace and direction caused me to be one of the top salesmen every single week. Again, it wasn't me doing it. It was because I had tapped into God's serving grace and obeyed Him. This anointing has made me better in every job He has called me to do, and it is available for every believer, so they can do what He's called them to do in this season of their life.

I remember this lady in our church who cooked by walking in her serving grace, and her food was amazing! Why? Because she did it unto the Lord! When someone does something unto the Lord, it's just that much better. So, whatever you're called to do, do it unto the Lord. If you're an accountant, account unto the Lord. If you're a cook, cook unto the Lord. Whatever it is, do it unto the Lord. When you do it unto the Lord, that is when you will be doing it in His grace and His ability.

In all my years of pastoring, I've been with many people who have gone home to be with the Lord, and the two things I have heard many times are, "I wish I would have fully obeyed God," and "I wish I had spent more time with my family." One has to do with obeying what God has called us to do, and the other has to do with loving God, loving others, and loving ourselves. That's God's purpose for us all.

God is offering all of us this enablement, so we can serve Him more abundantly in every area of our life; but if we only access His grace at church and not during the week, our week will be harder. This grace is there to help us make better decisions. The more of this grace we walk in, the more aware of this grace we'll become, and the better able we will be to recognize whether we're doing it in His strength, or on our own. I can tell when something is my bright idea and there's no grace to do it. How? It becomes hard to get it done because I'm trying to do it in my own strength. However, when it's a God idea, the grace is there enabling me to do it and somehow, it just all comes together.

When we built our offices and temporary youth room, it was God's idea; and even though there was opposition, and it seemed like the wrong time to build, the grace got it done. I saw so much grace on our Associate Pastor who was overseeing the build. I watched this grace on his life give him favor with so many subcontractors. They did things for him that they wouldn't do for anyone else. That's serving grace! This grace will give you the ability to do all you do with excellence and give you favor with man too. Access it and walk in it, so it can enable you!

The more grace we access and walk in for each area (salvation, living, standing, serving, finances), the more grace we can access as we build our faith, and then even greater grace will be revealed to us. We never have to settle because the good news is that there is always more grace available! The amount of grace we walk in today is the amount we've settled for, based on how much we have exercised our faith, so let's never settle. Let's use our faith and go for the more!

Not only can we obtain more grace, by faith, for the place we're currently in, but we can also obtain it for the new or temporary place God has called us to, like it was for our Associate Pastor who received grace when overseeing the building project. No matter what place we're in, the grace will be there according to the proportion of our faith. Now, when we do receive more grace, that usually means there will be more for us to do, but His grace is more than enough to handle it. God's Word, His grace, and the Holy Ghost leadings have brought each of us to where we are today; and as we continue to cooperate and walk in more of His grace, it will take us to where we're supposed to go.

God's serving grace, as it grew, radically changed Saul, who became Paul. Saul, who was killing Christians, met Jesus on the road to Damascus, and received mercy, because what he had done was in ignorance and unbelief. And even though Paul met Jesus that day, he didn't discover his grace until he grew his faith. In Acts 13, the Holy Ghost said, "Separate Barnabas and Saul (Paul) for the work I have called them to," which was as prophets and teachers. Paul had discovered his call, believed God, and then accessed His grace to teach the good news to the Gentiles. This grace was always there, but Paul had to receive faith to be able to access it. When he did, he later discovered another calling God had for him and that was to be an apostle (2 Timothy 1:11), for which he accessed more grace so he could do that too.

God's grace was also on Ananias to lay hands on Paul to restore his sight after he had been blinded on the road to Damascus. This blindness wasn't sickness or disease. It was the glory his eyes had seen. Ananias was also used of God to fill Paul with the Holy Ghost. These good works were assigned specifically to Ananias, in his mother's womb, to do, so he could help Paul get on the right track. I've often wondered why God didn't send an apostle to minister to Paul instead of Ananias, who was not an apostle, or even a prophet, or an evangelist, or a pastor, or a teacher. Ananias was just a regular guy who obeyed the Lord, and yet, he would forever be known by all for what he did for Paul. How awesome is that? It shows me that we all have good works that God has assigned to us to do, and we don't have to be behind a pulpit to be used mightily by God.

This grace is an empowerment to labor without getting worn out. If we try laboring without grace, we're doing it in our own, and we will find ourselves getting weary and wanting to give up. That's what the enemy wants. If he can wear us down, bring division, and separate those in the body of Christ, we will no longer remain strong as one body to bring in God's harvest; but if we will tap into His grace, we can labor more abundantly without growing weary because it's God's grace in us that will enable us to labor even more. That's what God's amazing grace will do. When someone says, "You're a great parent," or "You're a great worker," or "You're a great business owner," and so on, it's because God has graced them to do it, and they are walking in their grace by faith!

Are you receiving all the grace that God has made available to you? It's so important that you do, and only you, and God know if you are. Let's not miss any of the opportunities that God brings to us.

We need this grace more than ever because we're living in the last days. What if tomorrow, the trumpet sounded, the dead in Christ were raised, and you were caught up with Jesus in the air; and then the next moment, you were standing at the judgment seat of Christ? Are you ready? I remember some of my spiritual heroes saying, "One thing I do is I live every day like I'm about to stand before the judgment seat of Christ." That's how we should all live. When someone thinks they're about to stand before the Lord and hear about what they've done in their body, it'll make them live each day differently. When we appear before Jesus, we are only accountable for the grace He has given us, so as long as we keep doing what God has asked us to do, we will hear "Well done!" and receive our reward!

A Word for Ministers on Serving Grace:

Graces will differ:

Pastor graces are similar because of the pastor calling, but they differ as well because each pastor is different. They differ depending on the place they serve, the way they are called to pastor, and their natural differences. I am who I am, and you are who you are, by the grace of God, because God never intend for us to be the same.

Graces between senior pastors, although similar, differ too depending on the measure God has given based on their assignment, and the different ways this grace is manifested through them.

Graces for a senior pastor will differ from an associate pastor; and grace for a youth pastor will differ from a children's pastor. Our youth pastor has been in that office for over 20 years, which is unusual for a youth pastor to remain that long, but he is graced to reach that age. And now, I can see that his grace is changing, so he's trained other faithful men and women who have that same grace to move into this place. Our children's pastor has now been doing it for a few years, and you can clearly see her grace for that age group.

Because graces, though similar, are not the same, we should never compare our graces with each other. 2 Corinthians 10:12 says that we are not to compare ourselves among ourselves. "I am [uniquely] who I am" and so are you! And even though pastor graces differ, they are still supposed to work together because my grace is not greater than yours and your grace is not greater than mine. Each person's grace is important and necessary.

Some of the serving graces are found in Romans 12, which are:

- Prophecy
- Ministry
- Teaching
- Exhorting
- Giving
- Ruling

These graces will be expressed in different ways because of a person's specific call, and the grace endowments they are given based on their call. Even though God intends for each one of us to have certain graces (giftings), each person must grow in their faith to receive them and the amount they receive will be in proportion to their faith.

If prophecy, they will only prophesy in proportion to their faith.

If exhorting, they will only exhort in proportion to their faith.

If teaching, they will only teach according to the proportion of their faith.

The Apostle Paul, though graced from his mother's womb, still had to access the grace, by faith, before God could activate it, and only then, was Paul enabled to step into the office of a teacher, and then an apostle.

Everyone's grace is so unique, and that includes the children of ministers. Although God calls everyone, that doesn't mean that their children are called to be just like their parents because they have their own individual and unique graces. It would be a mistake to make their kids be like them because only God can make that happen. A parent's calling, and the graces that go with it, are not automatically passed down to their children. Grace is given by God and God alone. As a parent, I can't put the grace I have been given on my daughter. It's either there for her to access or it's not. I cannot put her in a position that God has not graced her to do. I've watched ministers do exactly this, and it ends in disaster and can even bring destruction to a ministry. Just like ministers follow God's calling on their life, their children must also follow the calling God has put on their life.

Be faithful to these graces (gifts of the Spirit):

Use the gifts you have been given to serve one another. Do you have the gift of speaking? Then speak as though God, Himself, were speaking through you. After you've spent the time preparing a message knowing you've heard from Heaven, believe you have something good to give and that His grace will bring it forth. Say this to build yourself up: "As I speak, I speak as a messenger of God; and I have grace to pastor these people." So now, when you get behind the pulpit to minister, your confidence will come from God because you know He's given you a word in due season that will refresh the weary.

So, how do you receive your ministry gift? The same way all grace is received, by faith. Believe and say: "I access, by faith, the ministry gift that God has ordained for me to have, and I walk in this gift based on the proportion of my faith." Accessing ministry gifts are always based on the amount of faith the person has, so grow your faith, which is done by hearing (and studying) the Word of God. The more we grow in faith, the more grace, concerning these ministry gifts, we can access, and there's always more grace available for us to receive.

Pastors are called to be a faithful steward over the spiritual endowments (gifts) given to them (1 Corinthians 4:2). When these gifts are used to serve others, it brings glory to God. Matthew 22:14 says, "Many are called, but few are chosen," is saying that it's up to us to position ourselves to be chosen. God is faithful to His Word, and He expects us to be faithful to what He has given us.

These ministry gifts are the true riches that God wants to give, but first, God will use money as a test of faithfulness before He will give His true riches. An example of this is found in Matthew 25 in the story of the talents. A master gave his three servants talents (money) to handle for him. He gave one servant five, the second servant he gave two, and to the third servant he gave one. The servant with five doubled it and so did the servant with the two. The master said to both these servants, "Well done, thy good and faithful servants. You've been faithful over a little. I will make each of you a ruler over cities." The third servant, who was given one talent, did nothing with it. This servant said, because his master was hard, he buried the talent to keep it safe. The master called this servant wicked and slothful. Then he took the servant's one talent and gave it to the servant who had doubled the five. This story teaches us that it does matter how we handle what we have because someone who can't even handle something as natural as money, won't be able to handle the spiritual endowments that God has for them.

When God calls someone to pastor, He will watch how they handle money, especially the money given to the church that they oversee. If they are not faithful in handling it with honor and integrity, it will hinder their anointing as a pastor. God is waiting for you to pass the money test before He will give you His true riches. In handling both money and spiritual endowments, I always ask myself, "Am I being faithful to what He has told me to do? Am I walking in the grace He has given me? Am I waiting on God for something He has already done?" It's so important for all of us to keep a check on ourselves, so that we do remain faithful.

The course we are on today is because of our obedience and faithfulness. God will place someone as the head of a ministry, not based on their talent and abilities, but because they have been a good steward of what they have already been given and knowing they will continue to grow in faith and in grace. The more grace we walk in, the greater results we will have in life, in our church and in our ministry. As we grow, we'll receive greater understanding of the vision God has placed in us and can then access the grace needed to do things we haven't even touched yet.

God always asks us to do things that we cannot do on our own. Why? He wants us to rely on Him because He is not willing to share His glory with anyone. And that way, with every success we have, we can honestly say, "Glory to God!" because it was God who did it! Amen!!

Be in tune with your grace:

Pastors can be graced to stand in multiple offices. So, if you know God has called you to another office, access the grace He has for that office as well, and then get to doing it.

When your grace seems to be changing, find out what that means by checking your heart and going to God in prayer. The Lord may start you out in one thing and then move you to something else, so let God show you where you are supposed to be and access the grace needed to take that next step.

This was a tongue and interpretation the Lord gave when I was teaching a group of pastors: "So, each and every one of you, I've called you. I've graced you, and I've anointed you. And as you rehearse my Word, and as you rehearse my assignments, then I will give you divine things from myself to you that will help you walk in the grace and in the calling that I have assigned to each and every one of you. So, come, let us spend time together. Bring me my Word and I will download instructions for each and every one of you."

God is just waiting for us to come to Him, so He can show us what He has for us. Be like the Apostle Paul, who didn't immediately consult with flesh and blood, but first, he firmly established in his heart what God had said to do. If you're not firm in what God has said, take it back to Him, so He can again download His instructions to you. Then, do it; and when you do, He will take care of everything that concerns you (Psalm 138:8).

Grow in faith to grow in grace:

It's all about walking in His grace and not in what we

128

think we know. I'm not a better pastor and teacher today based on what I know, my experience or the years I've been doing it. That is not what elevates or increases anyone. It's God who promotes and gives the increase according to the grace we have accessed and walked in by faith, but to receive more grace, we must grow in faith. It's okay for ministers to get help and counselling, but it should never be a substitute for walking in faith and accessing His grace, nor should it ever override what the Bible says, or the leadings of the Holy Ghost. Growing in the Word, and believing what it says, will bring us greater revelation and direction to do what God has called us to do. I'm a better pastor today and have increased in my ability to preach, teach, prophesy, give a tongue and interpretation, and minister to others because I grew my faith and expected more, which enabled me to access more grace.

I've watched so many, who love the Lord, not increase, and even decline in grace because they have tried to improve their craft instead of growing their faith to access more grace. Knowledge and experience are helpful, but in order to go higher in the things of God, our trust must be in His grace. It's only when we access more grace that we will truly have God's ability to be successful in the ministry. I determine each day, on purpose, to learn more of His Word and, by faith, I expect to grow in His grace, so I can go higher and help more people because I want to disciple and bring as many people to the Lord as possible.

Chapter 06

GRACE TO BE RICH

Another grace we can access by faith, is grace to be rich. The word "rich" shouldn't be a dirty word to believers. It's certainly what the world seeks after, but for them that means having lots of money. Being rich for a believer means having an abundant supply, always having enough. I remember how frustrated I used to get when I didn't have enough. Back then, I gave what I could; but now that I have grown my faith, this grace continues to abound in me, and that's what Jesus wants for every believer.

One of the areas the enemy messes with us the most is in our finances, but even though Satan is the god of this world and has a lot of control over this worldly system, he can't triumph over a born-again believer who knows and walks in the truth.

> *2 Corinthians 8:9 For ye know the grace of our Lord Jesus Christ, that, though he was rich, yet for your sakes he became poor, that ye through his poverty might be rich.*

Or you could say, "Jesus became poor, so we could have an abundant supply." How? Through His death, burial, resurrection, and ascension. Jesus paid for it all!

It says that Jesus became poor, so we could become rich. And yes, Jesus did leave heaven where streets are made of gold and came to the earth where streets are made of dirt, to be born as a baby having nothing, but this scripture isn't referring to that. It is talking about Jesus giving up His godly form and position to become human. He gave up everything, so He could give us everything.

2 Corinthians 8:9 is a foundational scripture in teaching on prosperity. Yes, I said, "Prosperity!" That's another word many consider to be evil when it comes to believers. The dictionary defines prosperity as the condition of being successful, thriving. God wants us to thrive, to be wealthy, healthy, and happy. Being wealthy doesn't necessarily mean becoming a billionaire, or even a millionaire, but it does mean having enough for our every need and helping with the needs of others.

Why does God want us to do well? So, we can be a

blessing to others, just like Abraham, our father in the faith. God told Abraham that He would be blessed and be a blessing to others (Genesis 12:2); and now, the blessing of Abraham belongs to us.

Galatians 3:13-14

[13] Christ hath redeemed us from the curse of the law, being made a curse for us: for it is written, Cursed is every one that hangeth on a tree:

[14] <u>That the blessing of Abraham might come on the Gentiles</u> through Jesus Christ; that we might receive the promise of the Spirit through faith.

The curse of the law is very real. Deuteronomy 28 has a long list of them. What is the curse? It is three-fold: spiritual death, sickness and disease, and poverty. The curse entered into the world after Adam and Eve sinned in the Garden of Eden; but the good news is that Jesus purchased us back with His own precious blood and redeemed us from the curse. That means that every time the enemy tries to bring a curse our way, we can say, "I've been redeemed from that." We can name the specific curse and say, "I've been redeemed from sickness," "I've been redeemed from poverty," "I've been redeemed from (whatever it is named)."

Jesus took the curse for us, and then made His grace available for us to be rich, because He wanted us to experience His abundance. I'm not trying to get rich.

Jesus already made a way for me to be rich, but it's up to me to access this grace and walk in it before I see His prosperity flowing in my life.

God wants us all to have an abundant supply and is delighted when we do. I find it funny that many people, including believers, are not okay with it, especially when it comes to preachers having an abundant supply. They think that keeping a preacher poor is how to keep them humble. Having things, or not having things, isn't what keeps us humble. Those are outward conditions. Humility is a heart condition. 1 Peter 5:6 says we must humble ourselves. I really don't understand why people think it's okay for movie stars to have a private jet, but not somebody who is preaching the gospel.

Many Christians have been taught that money is evil, but the scripture doesn't say that. It says, "The love of money is the root of all evil" (1 Timothy 6:10), so it's not having money but loving money that is evil. Why? Because when someone loves money, it becomes their master. No one can serve two masters, God, and money, because they will end up loving one and hating the other (Matthew 6:24). We are not to love money. We are to love and serve God.

Money is just meant to be a tool, like driving a car, or wearing cologne or perfume. My car gets me to where I want to go, and cologne makes me smell good, but there are people who have misused both. Some have misused their vehicle by driving too fast, or intentionally running someone over, while others have misused cologne or perfume by putting too much on. Just because they've misused these tools doesn't mean I'm going to stop driving or wearing cologne. There will always be those who will take the good and misuse it, but that is no reason for us not to partake of what God has provided, which includes prosperity, His grace to be rich.

Money is a great tool that we need to function in our daily lives, but it's a horrible God. How can we tell if money has become our God? It's when we make life decisions based on money, rather than being led by the Spirit. If money is the reason someone takes another job, or moves to another city, or even gets married, then they are being led by money, and not by God.

Is it wrong to have or want to have money? Absolutely not! That's what this chapter is all about, but we can't let money "have us" by letting it decide what we will or will not do. When we do that, we have let it take the place of God. We all want to be in the right place, at the right time, doing the right thing, but that can only happen when we make godly decisions, based on the Word of God and the leadings of the Holy Spirit. When we do, money will just naturally follow. Our life decisions have brought us to where we are today, and the decisions we make today will determine where we go tomorrow. So, when we have a big decision to make, we should pray, and ask God what we should do, then be led.

There are some who have misused and wrongly taught the "grace to be rich" message to deceive or pressure people into giving for their own selfish gain. That's not Bible, and those who do that are teaching a fake doctrine. We can't stop the fake, because where there is the real, someone will always come up with a fake. We see that happening in the world today with products like Rolex, Gucci, Prada, and so on. There are people who sell fake products of named brands to make money, but that doesn't make the true product any less real or less desirable.

Those who have mistaught on prosperity have definitely misused finances themselves, so we do need to be careful of them. When we hear the Word of God taught, we should always take it back to the Bible to make sure it agrees with what the Word says. If what they are teaching is not in the Word, they are teaching in error, and we shouldn't listen to them. Instead, we should only listen to those who are teaching what the Bible says, based on sound doctrine. That is what will truly grow our faith. There will always be those who will teach false doctrine for their own gain, but that doesn't mean that applies to all preachers, because it doesn't. We wouldn't throw the baby out with the dirty bath water, so let's not throw away the message of prosperity because of false teaching. Grace to be rich is part of the good news of the gospel and people need to hear it. God wants us to be rich and has provided His grace to enable us to get there.

His prosperity is real, and He wants His children to live abundantly while they are here on the earth, so don't let those who have taken this biblical message and twisted it for their own purposes keep you from walking in this grace. I believe if anyone is having a problem in the area of finances, this Word on grace to be rich in this chapter will set you free.

Faith always comes by hearing, and hearing by the Word of God. And even though I don't teach a lot on finances myself, I do have someone in every service spend 5-10 minutes during the offering teach on it. Why? So, people can grow their faith to receive this grace to be rich. When we truly understand the importance of giving, we will become abundant givers, and will see this grace increase on our life. 2 Corinthians, Chapters 8 and 9, have a lot to say about this grace. The Apostle Paul tells us how this grace was evident in the churches in Macedonia.

2 Corinthians 8:1-2 (NKJV)

[1] Moreover, brethren, we make known to you the grace of God bestowed on the churches of Macedonia:

[2] that in a great trial of affliction the abundance of their joy and their deep poverty abounded in the riches of their liberality.

This grace of abundance, this endowment, could be seen

in these churches, because they had become liberal givers. Even though they were quite poor, and it didn't look like they could give anything, they gave much from what they had.

2 Corinthians 8:3-5 (NKJV)

³ For I bear witness that according to their ability, yes, and beyond their ability, they were freely willing,

⁴ imploring us with much urgency that we would receive the gift and the fellowship of the ministering to the saints.

⁵ And not only as we had hoped, but they <u>first gave themselves to the Lord</u>, and then to us by the will of God.

It says, they first gave themselves to the Lord, and when they did, the grace to be liberal in their giving kicked in. That's when Paul sent Titus to minister to them even more about this grace.

2 Corinthians 8:6 So we urged Titus, that as he had begun, so he would also complete this grace in you as well.

This grace had already begun flowing there, but Titus came to give them more understanding of it, so this grace would increase in them all the more. It's not about God giving us riches, but empowering us with His grace, His ability to obtain riches. Titus had tapped into this grace through the revelation he had received and went to the Macedonian church to teach them how to tap into it too, so they could abound in this grace as well. We should all be abounding in this grace.

2 Corinthians 9:8 And God is able to make all
grace abound toward you; that ye, always
having all sufficiency in all things, may abound
to every good work.

God is able to make this grace abound to us. Start believing this grace has been made available to you, and that you always have all sufficiency in all things, so you can give into every good work. Then, as you keep God and His Word first place, and follow the leadings of the Holy Ghost, this grace will begin to abound in you!

It's natural for people to want this grace to abound, so they can get the latest, greatest car, or a bigger house, and so on, but that shouldn't be our first thought. If it is, our priorities are out of order. We should want this grace to abound in our lives, so we always have enough to give into every good work. To help keep our focus right, we need to continually remind ourselves of that. A good confession, and one we do in my church, is, "I am blessed to be a blessing."

God wants us to have nice things, as long as those things don't have us. He's okay with us having big houses, expensive cars, and whatever else we desire, but if He ever asks for any of them, be ready to give them away because when God asks us to do that, it's so He can give us more. When giving becomes our first priority, rather than having stuff, that's when God can give us all the things we desire. If this grace isn't working in our life, we won't have anything to give away to bless others and receive more from God. The Bible intends for us to be the lender and not the borrower (Deuteronomy 28:12). Our priority should always be on giving. This grace will compel us to want to give even more, and that's when God is able to give more to us.

There are those in the body of Christ who do have a special grace for giving more generously and more abundantly, because it is part of their calling, but that doesn't take the rest of us off the hook. All Christians are supposed to tithe and give; as a person of grace and of faith, we should desire to do both. Why? Because it is our corresponding action to what we believe. It is being a doer of the Word.

The Bible clearly tells us that the tithe is holy and belongs to the Lord (Leviticus 27:30), and that hasn't changed just because we are New Testament believers. What God said in the Old Testament still applies to us today.

Hebrews 7:1-2

[1]For this Melchisedec, king of Salem, priest of

*the most high God, who met Abraham returning
from the slaughter of the kings, and blessed
him;*

*² To whom also Abraham gave a tenth part of
all; first being by interpretation King of
righteousness, and after that also King of
Salem, which is, King of peace.*

Yes, this is the New Testament referring to the Old Testament, but Hebrews goes on to say that God has made Jesus a priest forever after the order of Melchizedek (Hebrews 5:6). The tithe is still in effect, just like the Ten Commandments still apply today, because when we walk in the New Testament law of love (love God and love others), we won't violate any of them. When we tithe and give offerings, we're obeying the Word and positioning ourselves to reap a harvest.

*Luke 6:38 Give, and it shall be given unto you;
good measure, pressed down, and shaken
together, and running over, shall men give into
your bosom. For with the same measure that ye
mete withal it shall be measured to you again*

We should always have a heart to give and to bless others because that's being a doer of the Word. Each time we give as the Lord directs, we are honoring Jesus. When we tap into this grace and walk in it, we too can become a liberal giver just like those in Macedonia. For anybody who is still living in poverty and doesn't see how they can give, ask God for seed (money) to sow (give).

2 Corinthians 9:10 Now he that ministereth seed to the sower both minister bread for your food, and multiply your seed sown, and increase the fruits of your righteousness.)

When someone has a heart to give, this grace will come on them, and somehow, they'll find a way to give, which will cause this grace to grow in them even more, so they can give more, and more, and more! Just believe God and start where you're at. Confess, "God gives seed to me because I am a sower," and then, when God does give you seed, make sure you take that seed and sow it, so you can reap a financial harvest. Don't eat your seed. What I mean by that is, if you've been praying for seed to sow, and then extra money comes to you, don't go spending it on yourself, because God provided it to you to give, so he could give you even more.

If anyone is having trouble seeing that it's God's will for them to have an abundant supply, they should renew their mind with the Word of God and confess what the Bible says about His abundance until they can see it for themselves. It starts with a desire, a want to give, and then believing what they give is important. Even the woman who gave the two mites, God made mention of her, because she gave it from the heart (Matthew 12:42:43). God wants to multiply your seed sown, so just remain faithful in giving what you have, and God will do His part.

It's all about cooperating with this grace and doing what the Word says, that causes this grace to flow abundantly in our life. Once we access this grace, by faith, and then walk in it by giving, this grace will grow in proportion to what we can believe (Romans 12:6). If we don't understand or cooperate with this grace, we can give, and give, and give, but we'll never reap the financial harvest we desire, because we will have sown with the wrong heart or the wrong motive.

Some people, when they hear this message taught for the first time, get excited about tithing and giving; but then, when they don't receive a quick return on their giving will say, "This doesn't work." Tithing and giving always works, so why didn't it work for them? The short answer is that instead of believing the Word and giving from their heart, they were trying to work it to get something, or their patience was lacking (Hebrews 6:12). We will never reap a financial harvest if our thinking is wrong, or we let go of our faith.

Until we have a greater revelation of this grace, our lack of knowledge will limit us. Start seeing this grace abounding in your life, and that you always have enough to give into every good work. When we believe this in our heart and are diligent in our giving, it will produce a harvest. It takes faith and patience to bring our harvest in, just like it does with a farmer, seed, time, and harvest. God wants us to have a harvest, but to receive it, we must sow, and to sow we must have seed (something to give), and then we must call our harvest in; finally, we must be patient for it to come since we don't know the length of time it will take between planting our seed and seeing our harvest because it is the Lord who produces the harvest of financial blessing and not us. So, until we see our harvest of giving, we must water our seed by meditating on the Word of God, and then use our sickle, which is our tongue, to bring in our harvest by confessing the Word over our seed sown (given).

Confession: "The grace of the Lord Jesus Christ is upon me, and, by that grace, I am rich."

God's grace will not only bring a blessing of increase, but it can also multiply this grace exceedingly!

2 Corinthians 8:1 And by their prayer for you, which long after you for the <u>exceeding grace</u> of God in you.

So, this exceeding grace can abound in us. Joseph abounded in this grace. Genesis 37 says Joseph had a coat of many colors that his daddy had given him because of his great love for Joseph. This caused Joseph's brothers to hate him because they were very jealous of him. Then, when Joseph told his family he had a dream that everybody would bow down and worship him, it made his brothers hate him even more. His daddy pondered what Joseph had said, but his brothers pondered how to get rid of him. They wanted to kill him but sold him into slavery instead. In the Old Testament, many times, the word "favor" is used in place of the word "grace," and Joseph definitely had this favor on his life, which shows us that even in the Old Testament, God wanted His people rich. No matter where Joseph went, he prospered because God was with him.

Genesis 39:2 And the Lord was with Joseph....

When the Lord is with you, there is favor! This favor on Joseph's life wasn't dependent on his position in life. Even when Joseph was sold into slavery, his Egyptian master, Potiphar, made him the overseer of his household, because he could see this favor on Joseph. Grace (favor) can be seen, so others should be able to see this grace on us too, just like Potiphar saw it on Joseph; and when they do, we also will be highly favored.

Genesis 39:3-6

[3] And his master saw that the Lord was with him, and that the Lord made all that he did to prosper in his hand.

[4] And Joseph found grace in his sight, and he served him: and he made him overseer over his house, and all that he had he put into his hand.

⁵ And it came to pass from the time that he had made him overseer in his house, and over all that he had, that the Lord blessed the Egyptian's house for Joseph's sake; and the blessing of the Lord was upon all that he had in the house, and in the field.

⁶ And he left all that he had in Joseph's hand; and he knew not ought he had, save the bread which he did eat. And Joseph was a goodly person, and well favoured.

The Lord caused all that Joseph did to prosper. Joseph found grace in his master's sight and served him, so this favor is not only with God, but with man too. Jesus had favor with God and with man. This grace can give us favor everywhere we go. Favor is not meant to be fair. Favor is an endowment from God when we believe and access it, and then obey what God says to do. When this grace, this favor is on our life, God can do things for us that He cannot do for others.

Joseph was prospering in Potiphar's house but then, when he wouldn't be seduced by Potiphar's wife, she lied about him, and he was thrown in prison.

Genesis 39:20 And Joseph's master took him, and put him into the prison, a place where the king's prisoners were bound: and he was there in the prison.

It's never good to go to prison, but God's favor put Joseph in the king's prison; then, even in prison, God gave Joseph favor with man.

Genesis 39:21-23

²¹ But <u>the Lord</u> was with Joseph, and shewed him mercy, and <u>gave him favour in the sight of the keeper of the prison</u>.

²² And the keeper of the prison committed to Joseph's hand all the prisoners that were in the prison; and whatsoever they did there, he was the doer of it.

²³ The keeper of the prison looked not to any thing that was under his hand; because the Lord was with him, and that which he did, the Lord made it to prosper.

Joseph had favor with the keeper of the prison, who put him in charge of overseeing the other prisoners, and again, whatever Joseph did, prospered. Then Genesis 41 says that Pharaoh had a dream, and because Joseph, by the help of God, was able to interpret it, Pharaoh took him out of prison and made him second in command in Egypt. Joseph walked in God's favor in Potiphar's house, in the prison house, and then in the king's house! Joseph had been made second in command in each house he was in. That's favor! That favor was there working whether he was currently a slave, a prisoner, or a leader of a nation.

It doesn't matter what we look like, our education, or where or how we were born, planned, love child or unwanted child, this grace is available for you. Psalm 105:19 says, "The Word of the Lord tried Joseph" (Psalm 105:19). What does that mean? Joseph knew God had called him to be great, but with all that was happening to him, it didn't look like it, so Joseph had to keep believing, trusting, and obeying God for it to come to pass. When we feel tried, or it looks like things aren't going as they should, if we will just keep believing and access this grace, and then hold fast to the Word of God, we will see the dreams God has given us come to pass too. If someone doesn't like where they're currently at, just keep walking and growing in faith. Believe for this grace, access it, walk in it, and watch what God will do!

In each place Joseph served, he prospered, and then he became very rich as second in command in Egypt and was able to bring his entire family to live there. Genesis 45:7 says that God sent Joseph ahead to save His people alive, and because of Joseph's obedience in serving, God was able to position him to fulfill his destiny. Joseph went from his father's house to Potiphar's house, to the prison house, and then to the royal palace. That is definitely what I call rising to the top! Joseph is included in what we call the "Hall of Faith" (Hebrews 11). That's what God's favor, His grace, will do, and it can do it for you!

The Word of God's grace will not only cause us to rise; it will also build us up and give us an inheritance.

> *Acts 20:32 And now, brethren, I commend you to God, and <u>to the word of his grace, which is able to build you up, and to give you an inheritance</u> among all them which are sanctified.*

What is our inheritance? For those who are sanctified, it's all the promises of God which are yes and amen in Christ Jesus. We don't have to covet what others have, because we are heirs and joint heirs with the Lord Jesus Christ (Romans 8:17). Paul said he had coveted no man's silver, gold, or apparel (Acts 20:33), which meant he didn't seek something belonging to somebody else. Paul made tents to have money for his necessities, and the grace of God was there for him to do that. Does that mean every preacher ought to make tents? Of course not. This was specifically what Paul did in the season he was in. The Bible says that a minister is worthy of his hire and a double portion (1 Timothy 5:17-18), and that means receiving a salary in the church.

Our focus should always be on giving, which is what Paul did when he chose to give of himself by making tents. The Bible tells us that it is more blessed to give than to receive.

> *Acts 20:35 I have shewed you all things, how*

> *that so labouring ye ought to support the weak,*
> *and to remember the words of the Lord Jesus,*
> *how he said, <u>It is more blessed to give than to</u>*
> *<u>receive</u>.*

So, based on this scripture, we need to change our thinking to, "When we give, we will receive, so we can give again." That is the heart of God and our Savior.

Jesus said, "Everything the Father has is mine and I will give it to you," (John 16:15). God has always been a giver, and He wants His children to be givers too.

God gave His best when He gave us Jesus. Jesus was the seed, and everyone who is born again is His harvest.

Let's let God's grace, His favor to be rich, abound in us; whether in the ministry, have a business, a career, a job, or run a household, we should all access His grace to be rich. In God's kingdom, we are not limited by our paycheck. Yes, we are to work, because the Bible says if we don't, we shouldn't eat (2 Thessalonians 3:10); working is our corresponding action to what God's Word says, but whatever work we do, we should do it unto the Lord, which means we should always do it as if we are working for the Lord. That's when God can bring promotions, bonuses, raises, deals, and blessings through others. I also believe that when we walk in this grace, God can also give us witty inventions and nifty ideas that will cause us to prosper in the middle of anything and everything going on, because with this grace, comes the spirit of wisdom too. God is unlimited in the ways He can bless us. Our part is to believe that God's favor surrounds us like a shield (Psalm 5:12), and that His grace is working in our lives. When we walk in this grace, obey the Word, and follow His leadings, we will see God's favor and His abundance show up on our behalf. This grace can take someone who is at the bottom to the top, just like it did with Joseph.

Even under the Old Covenant, we can see God's abundance. In the desert, God rained down manna from heaven each day to feed the children of Israel. He rained down so much that the people wanted to store it up, but they couldn't, because when they tried, the leftover manna spoiled. Why did God let it spoil? Because God was teaching them to take just what they needed for that day, and then trust Him that there would be more tomorrow. It is from this account that we get our saying, "Money is like dust; there will be more tomorrow." It's our way of saying, we trust God for today and we will trust Him for tomorrow and for every tomorrow that follows. When we trust God, there is no need to hoard or pile up what we get. Instead, we should have a heart to give what we have to others.

When God is calling someone to do something, but they don't have the finances to do it, that can mean one of two things is happening. Either God didn't really tell them to do it, or they don't yet have the faith to receive the money needed to do it. To find out which it is, they should seek God in prayer and ask Him to make sure. Then, if God still says to do it, they need to build their faith by hearing, studying, and confessing the Word of God on finances, and then acting on the Word by doing what He says, so they will be able to receive the money needed to do what God has called them to do.

It is by grace, through faith in the Word, that we receive, so we're not trying to get God to do something that He hasn't already done. We are righteous because He made us righteous. We can be healed because He healed us. And we can be rich because He became poor for us to be rich. If someone would ask God to do any of these things, He would say, "I already did." Knowing this and knowing that God chose to make you rich and has this grace waiting for you to receive it is what will set you free!

Jesus prayed, "Father, your will be done on Earth as it is in Heaven," (Matthew 6:10). In Heaven, there is no sin, sickness, or poverty because it is God's will that we be free from all of that, so if it's His will in Heaven, then it's His will while we are here on the earth. Luke 4:18 begins by saying, "The Spirit of the Lord is upon me, because he hath anointed me to preach the gospel to the poor." Gospel means good news and what would be good news to someone who is poor? That you don't have to be poor anymore. I'm so glad we don't have to pry anything out of God's hand, because His hand is already open (Psalm 145:16), and His will is for us to be rich.

When we tell others that God wants them rich, some will say, "Well, you know the Bible says that it's easier for a camel to go through the eye of a needle than for a rich man to enter into the kingdom of God." Let me help anyone who thinks this way. This verse is found in Matthew 19:24, and when you study it out, Jesus was saying that it's hard for those who cling to and trust in their riches to enter into the kingdom of God. Jesus said this when He was talking to a rich young ruler who had asked what he must do to have eternal life. Jesus first told him to obey the Ten Commandments, which the rich young ruler said he was already doing. But then, Jesus told him to sell all he had, give it to the poor, and follow him. This the rich young ruler wasn't willing to do because he loved having money. Instead of identifying himself in Christ, his money had become a big part of his identity. Money cannot be our identity. Our identity must be found in Christ, and our trust must be in Him alone. The rich young ruler couldn't do that, so he sadly walked away. That's when Jesus said how hard it was for someone who loves their money to be in the kingdom of God. Those who love money rather than loving God will find it very difficult to enter into the things of God.

Peter, who was listening to what Jesus had said to the rich young ruler, asked Jesus, "What about those who have given up everything to follow you?" Jesus said, "Everyone that has forsaken houses, or brothers, or sisters, or father, or mother, or wife, or children, or lands, for my name's sake, shall receive a hundredfold, and shall inherit everlasting life" (Matthew 19:29). God said that they would receive a hundredfold, and from this we can also see that Jesus wasn't against us having houses (plural), or things, because it is His will that we be blessed, so we can be a blessing; but if we, ourselves, are not blessed, we won't be able to bless others. If you had it on your heart to give someone $1,000 dollars today, could you do it? If you're blessed, you could; but in order to bless others, you have to be blessed first!

The more we understand that God wants us blessed and also understand the abundance He has for us, the more we will be able to walk in it. Have we all arrived in His abundance? Can we all give into every good work? Maybe not yet, but we should all be moving in that direction, so we are able to give into every good work and be a blessing to others. Let's believe for God's grace to be rich, so we can be a blessing!

God wants us to have abundance, but we have to keep it in perspective, so we won't go overboard and become greedy. We don't ever want to have dollar signs for pupils. The Bible says we're not supposed to be covetous or serve money. Money is supposed to serve us. That's God's wisdom giving us balance.

Whatever we do should never be based on money, even though money is an important tool that we all need. I've walked through the garbage dumps in countries where people eat whatever they can find because they're poor and hungry. It's demonic and no one should have to live that way, because that is not the will of God for them. I've had people say to me, "You shouldn't preach prosperity to them. That's an American gospel." What are they saying? They're saying they don't believe God can prosper those who are so poor. That's wrong thinking, because this gospel applies to every Christian, no matter where they are or how they live. If a part of the gospel doesn't apply to a certain country, then it shouldn't be preached anywhere. But the truth is, the gospel, this good news is for everyone, no matter where they live or what their circumstances are. This grace to be rich will work for every believer in every country around the world, if we will preach it, so that those who hear it can believe and access this grace, by faith, for themselves. I've seen it happen. I've seen people grab ahold of this message, step out in faith, and prosper.

I remember when I first started going overseas, as a minister, to places where they didn't have much, but they would still do their best to give us an offering. At first, it was hard for me to receive it, because I felt like I should be giving to them, but I knew it was important for them to give, so God could bestow this grace to be rich on them; their giving was their corresponding action, which gave God legal entrance to bless them. This grace is what they needed to get out of their poverty, and through the years, as we have received their offerings, I've watched their faith grow and their finances increase. What a joy that has been for me! The Bible is clear when it says in Galatians 6:7, "Whatsoever a man sows, he will also reap." What does that mean? If you only give a little, you'll only receive a little, but if you give much, you'll receive much. Giving "only a little" has nothing to do with the amount. It's when your heart wanted to give more but you chose not to, and giving much is giving all your heart desires to give, like the woman who gave the two mites. Although this was a small amount, it was much because her heart desired to do it, even though it was all she had. God will give the increase, but we choose how much we will reap by how much we sow.

Some Christians want to believe that this grace to be rich is not for all believers, and will say, "Giving is just not my grace," but that's not so, because not only was this giving grace on the churches in Macedonia, but it then spread to the Corinthian churches as well. When this giving grace is taught, it can get on all believers who hear it, if they'll let it! So, for someone to say, "It's not my grace," what they are really saying is, "I don't have the faith to do it." So, what do they need to do? They need to grow in faith concerning this grace to know that when they give, they will reap.

Paul wrote to the churches in Corinthians and commended them for abounding in faith, in utterance, knowledge, diligence, and love, but then he said that they should also abound in this grace of giving (2 Corinthians 8:7); and it was for this purpose, Paul sent Titus to them to teach on this grace, so it could begin working there also.

2 Corinthians 8:16-19 (NKJV)

[16] But thanks be to God who puts the same earnest care for you into the heart of Titus.

[17] For he not only accepted the exhortation, but being more diligent, he went to you of his own accord.

[18] And we have sent with him the brother whose praise is in the gospel throughout all the churches,

[19] and not only that, but who was also chosen by the churches to travel with us with this gift, which is administered by us to the glory of the Lord Himself and to show your ready mind.

This brother, that went with Titus to the churches in Corinth, must have walked in this same grace of giving and prosperity, so when he taught about this grace that was upon his life, it caused everybody who heard and received the message to rise up and begin to give as well. These two, Titus and a brother, were sent to teach on prosperity, because of the special anointing they had, which sounds to me like they had a greater revelation of Jesus being made poor, so we could be made rich. It was something they carried, and Paul wanted the churches in Corinth to catch it, so they could walk in this spirit of giving and receiving also. Paul understood that once they caught it by revelation, they could begin to reap a financial harvest from what they sowed.

Liberal giving is for everyone! And there are wonderful examples in the New Testament of those who gave in abundance.

- Mark 14:3-9 tells of the woman with an alabaster box filled with expensive perfume, who poured it on Jesus's feet to honor Him before He went to the cross. The religious leaders that were with Jesus didn't understand why she did this; and Judas, who later betrayed Jesus, thought she should have sold it and given the money to the poor instead of wasting it by pouring it out, but Jesus said that because this woman did this, she would always be remembered for what she had done.

- Luke 10:29-37 is the parable of the Good Samaritan who came upon a man who had been beaten, robbed, and left for dead. This Good Samaritan took care of him both physically and financially. He bound up the man's wounds and put him on his donkey, and then gave money to an inn keeper to care for the man until he was well again. This Good Samaritan gave abundantly and saved this man's life.

- Acts 9:36-42 tells of Dorcas, also known as Tabitha, who had a grace to give, but instead of giving money, she would make garments for those in need. This example shows us that giving isn't always financial. When Dorcas died, all the women cried showing all the clothes she had made for them. The women sent for Peter, and she was raised from the dead. Even though her grace to give isn't what raised her from the dead, it was what endeared her to everyone and led them to get Peter when she died.

It is always more blessed to give than to receive (Acts 20:35). Acts 4 and 5 tells the story of a couple, Ananias and Saphira, who did not believe this. Instead of flowing in this abundant giving, they tried to manipulate this grace and ended up paying dearly for it. It was during a time when there was a special move of grace from the Holy Ghost that enabled Christians to sell their houses and lands and bring the money to the Apostles, so that no church member would lack anything they needed. When Ananias and Saphira sold their property, they only gave a portion of it to the church, but then lied saying they were giving all they had received. When they did this, they both died instantly. It wasn't because of their unwillingness to give it all. It was because they had lied about it. No one was making them give anything, but when they did give, they chose to be dishonest about it by pretending to be something they were not, which was willing and abundant givers. By being deceptive, they made a mockery of God's grace and it cost them their lives. Whenever we give abundantly, more than our 10%, or give additional offerings, that's great, but it should always be because we are led or have a desire to do it. Don't ever let anyone pressure you into giving, even if everyone else is giving. Giving must be done from the heart and in obedience to God.

When we operate in this grace from our heart, it pleases God.

Philippians 4:10, 14-19 (NKJV)

[10] But I rejoiced in the Lord greatly that now at last your care for me has flourished again; though you surely did care, but you lacked opportunity.

[14] Nevertheless you have done well that you shared in my distress.

[15] Now you Philippians know also that in the beginning of the gospel, when I departed from Macedonia, no church shared with me concerning giving and receiving but you only.

[16] For even in Thessalonica you sent aid once and again for my necessities.

[17] Not that I seek the gift, but I seek the fruit that abounds to your account.

[18] Indeed I have all and abound. I am full, having received from Epaphroditus the things sent from you, a sweet-smelling aroma, an acceptable sacrifice, well pleasing to God.

[19] And my God shall supply all your need according to His riches in glory by Christ Jesus.

Operating in this grace of giving brings praise, glory, and honor to the Lord (2 Corinthians 9:12-15). There is something about this grace and our desire to give that causes our sacrifice to come up before the Lord as a sweet-smelling savor, which makes God well pleased, so I definitely want to operate, live, and walk in this grace, because I want to please God.

This grace is especially important for pastors because money is needed to operate and grow a church. It takes finances to pay staff, keep the church building running, and host events. So, if someone is called to pastor but their church is not prospering, why is that? Because this, like being born again, is not automatic. Pastors, like everyone other believer, still have to access His grace to be rich, and then, must obey the Word and the leadings of the Holy Ghost to see this financial blessing in their church.

If you're not currently walking in this grace, a good place to start is to read and study 2 Corinthians, Chapters 8 & 9 because it has a lot to say about finances. It says that God is able to make all grace abound to you, so you will be sufficient in everything, but you must first believe and then receive it for yourself and for your church. God wants pastors blessed, so that the people they minister to can also be blessed.

Start confessing…

Over yourself: "I have grace to be rich. It abounds to me. I have everything I need. I am all sufficient in all things and I am able to give to bless others and can give into every good work because this grace is abounding in me."

Over your church, "My church is blessed to be a blessing. We have all sufficiency. We can do everything the Lord calls us to do. We can reach out to the lost. We can feed the poor. We can help anybody who comes to us. We can have events. We can do all these things because grace abounds to my church. Amen."

When you can see what you're confessing in faith, it will happen.

Let me ask you, "If money wasn't an issue, and you could be anywhere in the world doing whatever you wanted to do, what would you do?" If your answer is, "I sure wouldn't be pastoring," then, I question whether you were ever called to pastor at all, or it could be that you have not stepped into the grace that came with your calling. I remember the first time someone asked me this question. The answer immediately popped up from my heart, and I said, "I'd be doing the same thing I'm doing in the same place I'm in, only bigger." Today my answer hasn't changed. It's still the same unless God calls me to a different place or Jesus returns. If money were no object, I would still live in Madison, Alabama, pastor Cornerstone Word of Life Church, and do all the things I'm doing now but in a much bigger way.

If God is calling you to do something, but you don't have the money to do it, only one of two things is happening. Either God isn't really telling you to do it, or you don't have the faith to receive the money needed for what He's asking you to do.

It's also important for pastors to receive a salary from their church no matter how small the church may be. Many times, when pastors first start a church, they tend not to take a salary because they are trying to stretch the finances they have in order to operate the church. They think that by not taking a salary, they are helping God out, but God doesn't need their help. He needs their obedience. A pastor should always take a salary because it's scriptural.

> *1 Timothy 5:18 Don't muzzle the ox that treads out the grain.*

1 Timothy 5:17 Let the elders that rule well be counted worthy of double honour, especially they who labour in the word and doctrine.

Even if it's small, pastors should take something. If you don't have a definite amount in your heart of how much you should take, just ask God how much, and He will tell you. For a pastor not to take a salary is a lack of faith. It's not about having faith that your congregation will give, but having faith in God that He will provide, so give God something to work with by taking a salary.

When I first started the church so many years ago, with few attending, the Lord told me to take $50 a month as a salary. Then, as the church began to grow, the Lord told me to take $50 a week, then $100 a week. I still had a full-time secular job at a clothing store because the church salary wasn't enough to pay my bills, and I sensed that it was what I was supposed to do. Then, one day, the Holy Ghost told me to cut my hours in half at my workplace, so I could have more time to pastor, but I didn't obey. Then, He told me again, but I still didn't do it because I couldn't see how I would pay my bills and eat. So, here I am, a pastor, this great man of faith, but I didn't have the faith to believe for the grace to go part time. So, what happened? My grace at the clothing store changed because I was no longer graced to work full time, and that's when things turned bad. Because the grace had lifted, the people I worked with started saying, "We don't like working with you anymore. You're so

164

grouchy. What's wrong? What happened to you? You used to be so friendly, so happy." Nothing was going right on the job or at the church where before everything had been beautiful and so wonderful. Thank God, I finally came to myself, asked the Lord to forgive me, obeyed and went part time. Once I put in my notice in for part time, three new families came to the church, and I was able to increase my salary and meet the needs that my full-time job had been meeting. Then, right before I met Pastor Rhonda, the Lord told me to quit my secular job, so I could pastor full time. I was quick to obey that time and started making $250 a week as a full-time pastor. It may not have been a lot, but it was enough to live on, and get married! What am I saying? If you will follow the leadings of the Holy Ghost and walk in His grace, by faith, God will be able to meet all your financial needs because you now have His grace working in your life.

Many years ago, this pastor, who was struggling financially, came to me for counseling hoping I could help him because I had an accounting degree. It wasn't my accounting degree that made the difference. It was the Word of God. The first question I asked him was, "Are you taking a salary from the church?" He said, "No, I can work. It's okay. I just want to bless the church," and I said to him, "No; you have to do what the Bible says." I then gave him the scriptures which showed him he should be taking a salary and then, I told him to go home and pray and ask the Lord the amount he should take each week. He did, and the Lord gave him an amount. He thought it was too much for the church to handle, so he only took half of what God said to take. And the amount he took as a salary was the same amount that the tithes in the church went up. He came back to me and said, "I was very stupid. I should've taken the full amount." So, eventually he did, and it all worked out.

We have to do it God's way, according to the Bible. When we understand that it's by grace, through faith, that we are able to walk it out and receive, it will stop us from trying to do it our way.

God wants pastors to be rich. Yes, I said "rich." Ministers need an abundant supply to reach the lost, feed the poor, and bless people, and that can only happen when we walk in this grace and do what God says. This is our corresponding action to what we believe and the grace we have received. So, if you are having trouble seeing yourself with an abundant supply, keep renewing your mind with the Word of God until you see yourself the way God sees you.

Being rich, doesn't mean you love money or will mishandle it. Are there pastors who have done that? Yes, and although that does happen, it still doesn't change what the Word of God has to say about finances. We shouldn't discount the "grace to be rich" message just because some are teaching it for their own gain.

What we should do is turn away from wrong teaching and stay with the Word that says, "Jesus became poor to make us rich." So, let's go after this grace to be rich that Jesus has made available for us and share it with others. In doing this, we will be giving glory and honor to God because we are obeying and walking in His Word.

Chapter 07

GRACE & GLORY

In the previous chapters, we talked about the different graces, God's power made available for us to be saved, live, stand, serve, and be made rich. In this chapter, I want to talk about His glory, the manifest presence of God that can come upon us when we walk in His grace.

Often times, under the old covenant in the Old Testament, the word "favor" is used instead of grace. Abraham, Noah, Joseph, and Moses, along with others, found favor with God. Favor, just like grace, is the power of God given to His people to enable them.

Psalm 84:11 For the Lord God is a sun and shield: <u>the Lord will give grace and glory</u>: no good thing will he withhold from them that walk *uprightly.*

The Lord gives His grace (power) to those who walk uprightly, which means those who obey and do what He says. We can also receive His glory. This glory is a substance, a heavenly material. Heaven is referred to as "Glory." When we received His saving grace to be born again, the glory of God came to live on the inside of us, but in this chapter, I want to talk about how His glory can come upon us.

When we were born again, God made us righteous, by His choice, and not because of anything we did.

> *2 Corinthians 5:21 For he [God] hath made him [Jesus] to be sin for us, who knew no sin; that we might be made the righteousness of God in him.*

It is from this righteous position, given to us by God, that we are able to access more of His grace to walk in, so His glory can come upon us.

We know that Jesus walked in grace and glory.

> *John 1:14 And the Word was made flesh, and dwelt among us, (and we beheld his glory, the glory as of the only begotten of the Father,) full of grace and truth.*

It says, "We beheld His glory," which means we saw the

glory on Jesus, who is the Word made flesh. It also says that when Jesus was on the earth, He was "full of grace and truth." We are made in the image of God, so we should be full of grace and truth, with the glory on us too.

We learn more about His glory during a conversation between God and Moses in the book of Exodus, Chapter 33.

> *Exodus 33:11 And the Lord spake unto Moses*
> *face to face, as a man speaketh unto his friend...*

They talked as friends, and in this conversation and seemed to be going back and forth a bit in what they had to say. Earlier in the chapter, because of their disobedience, the Lord had become very angry with the Israelites, calling them a bunch of stiff-necked people; so much so, that God didn't refer to them as "My people," but "The people."

> *Exodus 33:12 And Moses said unto the Lord,*
> *See, thou sayest unto me, <u>Bring up this people</u>:*
> *and thou hast not let me know whom thou wilt*
> *send with me. Yet thou hast said, I know thee by*
> *name, and thou hast also found grace [favor] in*
> *my sight.*

Moses was supposed to take the people into the land that the Lord had given them, but he first wanted to know if God was going with him; so, he approached God from his position of favor, as a friend of God, and said, "You want me to bring 'this people' up, but You haven't told me who's going with me." Just like Moses, we need His presence to go with us wherever we go.

Moses then said:

> *Exodus 33:13 Now therefore, I pray thee, if I have found grace in thy sight, shew me now thy way, that I may know thee, that I may find grace in thy sight: and consider that this nation is thy people.*

Moses is now asking God for more grace (favor). I love their conversation and the relationship Moses had of being a friend to the Lord Almighty, because Moses wasn't perfect, and that shows me we don't have to be perfect either before we draw near and fellowship with the Lord. Moses then asked God to consider "this people" as "His people."

Today, we are God's people and have this same favor with God that Moses had. Jesus had favor with God and man (Luke 2:52), and so do we, because we are in Him. God also called Moses His friend, and we are too, because Jesus said of us, "I no longer call you servants, but I call you friends" (John 15:15). How great is that? And under the new covenant, we have it even better because in 2 Corinthians 6:18, God said, "And I will be a Father unto you, and ye shall be my sons and daughters." So, we're not only a friend of God, but we are family too!

God responded to Moses:

> *Exodus 33:14 And he said, My presence shall*
> *go with thee, and I will give thee rest.*

Moses had gotten what He wanted. God was going with him, and Moses even made it very clear in the next verse, that he didn't want to go without Him.

> *Exodus 33:15 And he said unto him, If thy*
> *presence go not with me, carry us not up hence.*

Moses saying that to God may sound arrogant to some, but Moses was talking to God as a friend would talk to another friend, and God's response was basically, "OK, I'll go with you." Moses continued:

> *Exodus 33:16-17*
>
> *16For wherein shall it be known here that I and*
> *thy people have found grace in thy sight? is*
> *it not in that thou goest with us? so shall we be*
> *separated, I and thy people, from all the people*
> *that are upon the face of the earth.*
>
> *17 And the Lord said unto Moses, I will do this*
> *thing also that thou hast spoken: for thou hast*
> *found grace in my sight, and I know thee by*
> *name.*

Moses wanted all to see that God was with them, so all would know they belonged to God. That's a good way for every Christian to live. When God goes with us, all will see that we are His. We shouldn't want to do anything without His presence. Yes, He lives in us, but we also need the manifest presence of God on us, because it's His glory that will change lives, and churches too. People should be able to see the glory of God on His sons and daughters.

Moses was really feeling good that God was going with him, so he boldly went a step further.

> *Exodus 33:18 And he said, I beseech thee, shew me thy glory.*

That was confidence speaking. I pray that we would walk in this same confidence with God that Moses did, and the following verses say we can.

> *1 John 5:14 And this is the <u>confidence</u> that we have in him, that, if we ask any thing according to his will, he heareth us.*

> *Hebrews 4:16 Let us therefore <u>come boldly</u> unto the throne of grace, that we may obtain mercy, and find grace to help in time of need.*

God then responded to Moses' confidence.

> *Exodus 33:19 And he said, <u>I will make all my</u>*

> *goodness pass before thee, and I will proclaim*
> *the name of the Lord before thee; and will be*
> *gracious to whom I will be gracious, and will*
> *shew mercy on whom I will shew mercy.*

God said He would make all of His goodness pass before Moses, but Moses didn't ask to see His goodness. Moses wanted to see God's glory. Did God change the subject? Not at all, because from this scripture we can see that the goodness of God is the glory of God. His goodness is part of the manifestation of His glory. Where God is, the glory will be there, along with His goodness, mercy, grace, and abundance!

In this same verse, God said, "I will proclaim the name of the Lord." Who is God talking about? He's talking about Jesus, and then followed that by saying, "I will be gracious to whom I will be gracious and will show mercy on whom I will show mercy." Thank God He chooses to be gracious and merciful to us, His children.

So, God is going to show Moses His goodness (glory), but only in the way that Moses could behold it.

> *Exodus 33:20 And he said, Thou canst not see*
> *my face: for there shall no man see me, and live.*

God was saying that although He and Moses could talk face to face while He was in the glory cloud, Moses couldn't actually see His face and live, because God's immense power of glory would be too much for Moses to see with his eyes and live.

> *Exodus 33:21 And the Lord said, Behold, there*
> *is a place by me, and thou shalt stand upon a*
> *rock.*

God put Moses upon a rock. This is our place too. Believers now sit in this place, which is at the right hand of the Father, where Jesus sits because Jesus is the rock.

> *Exodus 33:22-23*
>
> *22 And it shall come to pass, while my glory*
> *passeth by, that I will put thee in a clift of the*
> *rock, and will cover thee with my hand while I*
> *pass by:*
>
> *23 And I will take away mine hand, and thou*
> *shalt see my back parts: but my face shall not be*
> *seen.*

We stand on the rock, Jesus Christ, who is the Chief Cornerstone, and the revelation of Him and what He's done. It's in Him that we live and move and have our being (Acts 17:18). It's to that place we've been raised up together with Jesus Christ to sit (Ephesians 2:6).

It's important to know where we are seated, especially when fiery trials come.

> *1 Peter 4:12 Beloved, think it not strange*

concerning the fiery trial which is to try you, as though some strange thing happened unto you.

Fiery trials come from the enemy, but it says don't think it strange when they come, because they come to everybody. What are we to do when they come?

1 Peter 4:13-14

[13] But rejoice, inasmuch as ye are partakers of Christ's sufferings; that, when his glory shall be revealed, ye may be glad also with exceeding joy.

[14] If ye be reproached for the name of Christ, happy are ye; for the spirit of glory and of God resteth upon you: on their part he is evil spoken of, but on your part he is glorified.

Instead of getting into this "we're going to war!" attitude, we should rejoice when fiery trials come, because the Spirit of God and His glory is upon us. When we are walking uprightly, and people start speaking badly about us (fiery trial) or come against us (fiery trial) because of Jesus, just rejoice knowing we have become "partakers of the same sufferings that Christ endured," and, "Happy are we, for the Spirit of glory rests on us."

The next verse issues a warning that not all who are suffering will bring the glory.

*1 Peter 4:15 But let none of you suffer as a
murderer, or as a thief, or as an evildoer, or as
a busybody in other men's matters.*

When someone brings suffering to themselves because
they are murderers, thieves, evildoers, or busybodies,
there is no glory or grace upon them, because this was of
their own doing and not for Christ's sake. Believers who
are doing this, need to repent and get forgiven, so they
can get back to walking in the grace and glory of God. It
is only when we suffer for Christ's sake that the glory
will come.

*1 Peter 4:16 Yet if any man suffer as a
Christian, let him not be ashamed; but let him
glorify God on this behalf.*

We do have to resist steadfast in the faith and speak the
name of Jesus, but the first thing we should do is rejoice,
because we know our end is victory, and the Lord has
won the battle. That's when we will see the fiery trial
(the weight of the enemy) brought to crush us, be crushed
by God's glory when His power comes.

Philippians 4:4 says, "Rejoice in the Lord always!" That
means we can continue to rejoice during a fiery trial,
because God is with us and has given us weapons that
win. When we rejoice in the Lord, it will confuse the
enemy because he thinks he's got us right where he
wants us, but God... So, no matter what is coming at you,

there is always a "But God!"

> *Matthew 19:26 With men this is impossible; <u>but with God all things are possible</u>.*

> *Psalm 73:26 My flesh and my heart faileth: <u>but God is the strength of my heart, and my portion for ever</u>.*

There are many more "But God" scriptures in the Bible to encourage us. Just search for "but God scriptures" online.

The enemy thought he could take Jesus out, but God! 1 Corinthians 2:8 says, "If they had known, they never would have crucified the Lord of Glory!" The enemy soon realized his mistake when the Glorious One, Jesus, rose from the dead, and dispersed His glory to the apostles; then to the 3,000 who were saved; then to the 5,000 who were saved; and then to the multitudes. His glory is still being dispersed today to every born-again believer, so they can go into all the world and preach the good news of Jesus Christ, and see the glory dispersed to everyone who will believe and receive Jesus as Lord.

There is always a "But God" when the enemy comes, so rejoice. When the enemy tells you he's going to get you, rejoice! When he says he's going to destroy your business, rejoice! When he says you're not going to make it, rejoice! It may not always make sense to rejoice, especially to those around us, but we can, because we know the devil is a liar, and in Christ, we will win!

What else should we do when problems come? First, we need to understand that problems never come from God. God doesn't bring problems. The second thing is to know what brought the problem, so we will know how to deal with it. I've discovered there are three types of problems, which I call storms.

1. <u>Storms we create</u>. An example of this is Jonah who was thrown off the ship and ended up in the belly of a whale. This storm came because of Jonah's disobedience. God had told him to go to Nineveh and tell them to repent from their wickedness, but because Jonah disobeyed and wouldn't go, it opened the door to trouble. Once he repented and said he would obey, God was able to deliver him from his problem; and because Jonah went to Nineveh and prophesied what God had said, the people repented, and the city was saved.

<u>Remedy</u>: If you caused the storm, repent, and get back into obedience.

2. <u>Storms people around us cause</u>. That's what happened to Paul when he sailed to Rome. Paul even told them there would be trouble if they

sailed, but they wouldn't listen and then, an actual storm came. Paul prayed and God showed him what needed to be done. Paul then told the Centurion of the ship what to do, and although they were shipwrecked, everybody on the ship was saved. Paul even told them, "You should have hearkened to me" (Acts 27:21). Today we would say, "I told you so."

Remedy: If the storm is caused by someone else, pray and ask God what you should do to escape this storm.

3. Storms the enemy brings. This is like the storm that suddenly came up when Jesus and the disciples were going to the other side (Mark 4:35-41). A demonic storm arose that was meant to kill them, but Jesus used His authority and quieted the storm by rebuking the wind and saying to the sea, "Peace be still." The wind ceased and there was great calm again.

Remedy: If the storm is from the enemy, use your authority and command it to stop in Jesus' name.

Storms come to attack our mind, body, finances, family, job, and career. No matter the storm we face, there is always a "But God" and He will deliver us from them all when we obey, pray, and use our authority.

His glory or presence in us, can come upon us when we walk uprightly in His grace. Part of that is doing what 1 Peter 5 says.

1 Peter 5:7-9

[7]Casting all your care upon him; for he careth for you.

[8]Be sober, be vigilant; because your adversary the devil, as a roaring lion, walketh about, seeking whom he may devour:

[9] Whom resist stedfast in the faith, knowing that the same afflictions are accomplished in your brethren that are in the world.

We are to cast our cares on Him, we are to be sober and vigilant, and we are to resist the enemy steadfast in the faith. Steadfast means we keep resisting, and we don't stop. Why? Because if we do, the enemy, like a prowling lion, will devour us. 1 Peter 5:9 is a great reminder that we are not the only one having to resist, because the enemy tries to bring afflictions to every born-again believer. The next verse is where I want to get to, which says:

1 Peter 5:10 But the God of all grace, who hath called us unto his eternal glory by Christ Jesus, after that ye have suffered a while, make you perfect, stablish, strengthen, settle you.

It says we have been called to His eternal glory. This glory is not referring to when we get to Heaven, but to the Shekinah glory, the manifest presence of God, that is here for us today. It's the same glory Moses saw when God let all His goodness pass by. When the devil comes with weights, problems, or whatever it might be, the God of all grace will manifest His presence, His glory, on our behalf.

Then it says, "after we have suffered awhile." Yes, I said suffer, but just for a while. Suffering and dealing with problems didn't stop when we got born again. The Bible doesn't promise that. Suffering isn't something we get excited about, but we can get excited that God will deliver us out of whatever it is (Psalm 54:7); and through it, He will perfect, establish, strengthen, and settle us, because we have resisted the enemy steadfast in the faith.

So, be encouraged, knowing we can resist the enemy when he comes, and that it will only last for a short time, because we are seated in glory at the right hand of God; and it's God's glory that will put an end to what the devil is trying to do.

Grace and glory always work together.

Roman 5:2-3

[2] By whom also we have access by faith into this <u>grace</u> wherein we stand, and rejoice in hope of the <u>glory</u> of God.

> *³ And not only so, but we <u>glory in tribulations</u> also: knowing that tribulation worketh patience.*

It says we are to glory in tribulations. Tribulations! Here we go again. First fiery trials, then suffering, and now tribulations? Yes, they do come, but we have to look at them as the fiery trials they are, and by grace, stand against them, because we know that God's glory will be manifested. That is so opposite to our natural thinking, but we were not called to walk by our senses. We were called to walk in the spirit by faith.

So, it's time to glorify God when the devil comes, because we know that God is bigger than anything that tries to come against us. When the enemy tries to steal, kill, or destroy us, we can glorify God as we watch Him bring the victory. Then, through whatever the tribulation is, God will work patience in us. It goes on to say…

Romans 5:4-5

> *⁴ And <u>patience</u>, experience; and <u>experience</u>, <u>hope</u>:*

> *⁵ And hope maketh not ashamed; because the love of God is shed abroad in our hearts by the Holy Ghost which is given unto us.*

This patience will then bring experience which will bring hope, which will make us unashamed, because of the love of God we have in us.

So, when the devil comes, we are to stand in the grace of God we have accessed by faith and rejoice in the hope of His glory, knowing this will work in our favor, because God will always cause us to triumph (2 Corinthians 2:14). It is our faith that gives us the victory that overcomes the world (1 John 5:4), and greater is He that is in us than he that is in the world (1 John 4:4).

God wants us to grow in the knowledge of His glory.

> *2 Corinthians 4:6 For God, who commanded the light to shine out of darkness, hath shined in our hearts, to give the light of the knowledge of the glory of God in the face of Jesus Christ.*

In the latter days, this glory will cover the earth like the waters cover the sea. Before I went to Bible School, I experienced the glory. I was in a large church in Rio de Janeiro where my spiritual mother was preaching during a youth conference, and for the first time, I saw the manifest presence of God. There were a couple thousand teenagers in attendance, and they began to fall out in the Holy Ghost on a concrete floor, with no usher to catch them. The power of God was so strong in the room. It was amazing! I had seen God move and had experienced His glory!

From that moment on, I wanted to know more about the glory. It wasn't long after that happened, that I went to Bible school, and I remember this guest minister got up and said, "Today, the title of my message is 'The Spout Where the Glory Comes Out.'" I got so excited, because I'd been asking the Lord about the glory, how to find it, and what I had to do to get it, and how to get under it. That preacher rambled on for an hour and never mentioned the glory. Afterwards, I got in my car, and I was so mad. I know I shouldn't have been, but I wanted to know about the glory, and that teacher didn't tell me anything about it. As I was driving, I began talking to the Lord saying, "Lord, that man teased me. He knew where the glory spout was, and he didn't tell me." The Lord said to me, "You're the spout." I responded, "No, I need to find out where that place is, and what I've got to say and do to get it," and God said again, "You're the spout." Then He said it a third time, and I said, "No, not me." But it was me. I learned that day that I was the spout where the glory comes out, because we, as Christians, carry this treasure in us, so when we speak His Word or lay hands on someone, His glory is attached to it.

2 Corinthians 4:7 But <u>we have this treasure in earthen vessels,</u> that the excellency of the power may be of God, and not of us.

I believe even a greater knowledge of the glory of God is coming to the body of Christ, and as we learn and understand more about His glory, it will fill the earth.

In the Old Testament, the glory of God lived in the ark

of the covenant, but today, we are His temple, the gathered presence of God. God has chosen to no longer live in things made by man's hand, but to live in us. We, as Christians, are now the carrier, the tabernacle of the glory of God.

> *2 Corinthians 4:11 For we which live are*
> *always delivered unto death for Jesus' sake, that*
> *the life also of Jesus might be made manifest in*
> *our mortal flesh.*

Let the life of God that is within you, manifest in your life. Let His life, His power, the same power that raised Jesus Christ from the dead, quicken your mortal body. Let the life of Jesus manifest in your mortal flesh (2 Corinthians 4:11), so that His abundant grace might superabound in you to the glory of God (2 Corinthians 4:15). Let the zoe life work on the inside of you.

In between 2 Corinthians 4:7 and 4:11, it says...

> *2 Corinthians 4:8-10*

> *8 We are troubled on every side, yet not*
> *distressed; we are perplexed, but not in despair;*

> *9 Persecuted, but not forsaken; cast down, but*
> *not destroyed;*

> *10 Always bearing about in the body the dying of*
> *the Lord Jesus, that the life also of Jesus might*
> *be made manifest in our body.*

The enemy's attacks that come are meant to trouble us by causing distress and despair and are meant to persecute and destroy us. That's why God wants to manifest and display His glory, His power through us, so problems don't keep us down. It reminds me of these little toy people sold long ago called "Weebles." They were in the shape of a fat egg and weighted at the bottom, so when they fell over, they would come right back up. Their slogan was, "Weebles wobble, but they don't fall down." Even when things knock us down, if we will focus on the glory of God on the inside of us, His power will keep us from staying down. When our hope is in Him, the glory of God, the very power and life of God on the inside of us will keep us standing. Let His glory manifest in your life, in your home, in your business, and at your workplace, so you can continue to stand while the power of God is working on your behalf.

His glory will bring you favor, healing, and victory. His glory working through you will give you the abundant life He has for you. His glory will give you heaven on earth. A lot of Christians, who are going to Heaven, are not experiencing this heaven on earth, because they are not meditating on the Word to know what God has said or are not believing the truth of God's Word. If we don't know or believe the truth, then any lie will do. That's when the devil will lie to us morning, noon, and night, saying things like, "Healing is not for today," or "The only way to be rich is by work and the sweat of your brow." If you don't know the truth, you will believe these lies and do without. Not knowing the truth will keep us from walking in the promises of God. And if we don't know who is bringing it, or we think, "Whatever happens is either God doing it or He's allowing it," then we won't fight. That is Old Testament thinking during a time when they didn't have the revelation and authority that New Testament believers have. Jesus tells us very clearly in John 10:10 who is doing it.

John 10:10 The thief [Satan] cometh not, but for to steal, and to kill, and to destroy: I am come that they might have life, and that they might have it more abundantly.

It's Satan, the father of lies, who steals, kills, and destroys. When Adam and Eve sinned and turned the earth over to the devil, Satan became the god of this world (2 Corinthians 4:4). Jesus even called him the prince of the power of the air (Ephesians 2:2). The devil is here, but Jesus said, "I've come that you might have life more abundantly," and the devil can't stop that from happening unless we let Him. So, every time anything tries to take (steal, kill, destroy) from you, it comes from the enemy. There are no exceptions. The enemy is always the source, the root of it. Anything that messes with your family, home, business, or anything else, it's the enemy doing it.

The Lord and the devil are not on the same team. The

devil is not His hired assassin. God doesn't use the
enemy as His henchman. If it's good, it's from God. If
it's bad, it's from the devil. If it's life, it's from God. If
it's death, it's from the devil. God doesn't bring bad
things to teach us. God uses the Word to teach us and
will give us the victory when bad things do come, if we
will walk by faith, trust in Him and be doers of the Word.
Let His abundant grace abound in you, so the glory of
God will come.

> *2 Corinthians 4:15 For all things are for your
> sakes, that the abundant grace might through
> the thanksgiving of many <u>redound</u> to the glory of
> God.*

The word "redound" in the Greek is
"perisseuo," and it means to superabound (in
quantity and quality), to be in excess, exceed,
excel, increase, over and above.

> *2 Corinthians 4:17 For our <u>light affliction</u>,
> which is but for a moment, worketh for us a far
> more exceeding and eternal weight of <u>glory</u>.*

Yes, afflictions come, but this verse says they are light
and but for a moment. We all go through things, but they
don't have to last when we hearken to the voice of the
Lord. The Apostle Paul went through much affliction,
but rejoiced because he knew it would bring glory to God
when God's power was revealed to bring the victory.

Paul said, "I rather glory in my infirmities, that the power of Christ may rest upon me because when I am weak, God is strong (2 Corinthians 12:9-10). Paul understood that God's strength was made perfect in his weakness, because that's when the power of God could come upon Him. When we resist the affliction that comes our way, it will work a far more exceeding and eternal weight of glory in us.

Every time we resist, we get stronger! In the natural, it isn't easy to take pleasure in our weaknesses, because when problems come, what we want to do is recoil. Instead, we have to stand against them, so the glory of God can come upon us. That's a high level of faith, but the more we resist, the greater our faith will become as we strive for and grow in the revelation that Paul had, where we too can say, "I glory in my weaknesses."

> Confession: "When I am weak, I am strong in Him. I resist the devil because I believe the weight of God's glory that is in me is manifesting the power and very life of God in this situation. I'm getting stronger because the grace of God is multiplying and growing in me. God is quickening me, so I can stand, and I will see the victory!"

My challenge to you is that the next time trouble comes your way, before you do anything else, rejoice. Make the devil wonder what you're up to, because he just gave you his best shot and instead of it knocking you down and keeping you down, you're rejoicing. Continue to rejoice as you stand in His grace and resist the enemy, because that's when you will see the glory of God come upon you and bring your victory!

I love to minister on the glory of God. We've arrived in the last days, and we were born for this time, so don't get upset when you hear about wars, rumors of wars or plagues because the Lord said these things would happen in the last days. We have arrived at the greatest time in the church age. Jesus is coming back soon, not for a weak, wimpy, hiding in caves church, but for a glorious church, a church with the glory on it! The Lord is coming back for His harvest, and we are a part of that. You have come into the kingdom for such a time as this, so rise up like Esther did when God used her to save His people. Let God use you to bring in His harvest!

In these last days, there has to be a distinction between the church and the world. The church, for so long, has tried to be like the world to win the world, but that really hasn't worked. In order to win the world, we've got to be different. We've got to walk in righteousness, holiness, and sanctification just like Jesus did.

I've been teaching on the glory and the presence of God for over 30 years. I get excited about the glory, because when His presence comes, His power comes with demonstrations following. The Bible isn't just a bunch of thoughts written down. It's alive, and it's working! It was never meant to be a book of religion, but to draw us into a relationship with the living God who performs His Word preached. His Word will bring His power! Believe and speak His Word and watch what happens! It reminds me, back in the day, when a salesman would come to someone's house to sell a vacuum cleaner. They would immediately pour a bunch of dirt on the person's carpet, so they could demonstrate how good their product worked, so they could make the sale. In the same way, God is a demonstrator of His Word, and He desires to show us His glory and His goodness.

God is so good! He has blessed us with so much. I am blessed to be a blessing. He has given us favor. I'm highly favored. The same favor that surrounded Jesus surrounds us. He has given us goodness and mercy. His goodness and mercy shall follow me all the days of my life (Psalm 23:6). I can't earn anything of this. I can only believe, receive, and walk in it.

Father God and Jesus decided that while we were still on the earth, they would give us a taste of heaven. Deuteronomy 11:21 says, "Days of heaven upon the earth." Jesus, when He was on the earth, even prayed, "Father, your will be done on earth as it is in heaven," (Matthew 6:10). Praying God's will be done on earth as it is in heaven is what we all want, because there's no crime, no plagues, no fighting, no segment against segment, no language group against language group, no culture against culture in heaven. Why not? Because in heaven, God is in charge. Jesus prayed this way because God is not in charge of the earth. I know religion teaches that He is, but if God were in charge down here, He's not doing a very good job. We need to get the blinders off our spiritual eyes and get rid of any wrong religious teaching like, "It's all up to God," or "Whatever will be will be." 2 Corinthians 4:4 clearly says, "Satan is the god of this world," but the good news is he doesn't have to be our god, because Psalm 115:16 says, "The heavens are the Lord's, but the earth He's given to the sons of men." We live in the earth and even though God is not in charge, Jesus has given us authority over the enemy, so we can still have heaven on earth. This authority and all that God offers comes from a place of grace, so it's now up to us, who are born again, to receive the grace we need to walk in victory over the enemy.

I believe we are heading into the glory days, and greater days of heaven upon the earth (Deuteronomy 11:21). For many, the last days will seem scary, but for a believer, who knows the Word and walks uprightly before the Lord, they will be like it was for God's people in the land of Goshen. The plagues that came to Egypt did not come to God's people there, and that's how it will be for us.

The glory of God is the absolute power of God in demonstration. When the glory of God comes, things change. When the children of God were all in unity and one accord saying, "For the Lord is good and His mercy endures forever," the cloud (presence of God) came (2

194

Chronicles 5:13-14). Today, we've got something better than the cloud. We've got Him living on the inside of us. The things of the spirit should be so much more real to us than the natural things we see, hear, taste, smell or feel. We're from another realm; we are aliens just passing through. Our citizenship is in heaven, and our seat is in glory. When we let His Spirit rest on us, God's glory will come.

> *2 Corinthians 4:18 While we look not at the things which are seen, but at the things which are not seen: for the <u>things which are seen are temporal</u>; but the things which are not seen are eternal.*

Remember, the things we see and the problems that come are just temporary, so live each day in the eternal, and walk uprightly in His grace, so His glory can manifest in your life!

Chapter 08

GRACE WARNINGS

In this book, we have talked about five different areas of grace.

- <u>Saving grace</u>: Ability to be born again and receive all salvation includes safety, rescue, healing, protection, deliverance, doing well, being preserved, and made whole.

- <u>Standing grace</u>: Ability to stand against the devil and whatever he brings.

- <u>Serving grace</u>: Ability to walk and finish the course God has prearranged for us, and to serve where God has called us.

- <u>Grace to be rich</u>: Ability to have an abundant supply to give into every good work.

- <u>Living grace</u>: Ability to live each day righteously and victoriously.

In this chapter, I want to talk about some of the warnings, alerts to impending danger, God has given us concerning grace. A warning can apply to a specific grace or to all of them. When we see a warning in the Bible, the content of the chapter should reveal which grace, or graces, this warning is talking about.

Whenever we see a warning, it should be a red flag to slow down and see what God is saying to us, just like we would if we saw a warning sign on the road.

There are five grace warnings I want to talk about.

1. Do not receive God's grace in vain.
2. Do not frustrate God's grace.
3. Do not fall from God's grace.
4. Do not fail God's grace.
5. Do not insult God's grace.

1. Do not receive God's grace in vain.

2 Corinthians 6:1 We then, as workers together with him, beseech you also that ye <u>receive not the grace of God in vain</u>.

This verse is talking about saving grace, but to receive God's grace in vain applies to all His graces. "In vain" means to no end, without success or result.

Other translations say,

- Do not receive it to <u>no purpose</u> (AMPC)
- Do not <u>ignore</u> it (NLT)
- Do not <u>let it be wasted</u> (GNT)
- Do not <u>squander</u> it (MSG)

So, we are not to receive His grace in vain, to no purpose, or ignore, waste, or squander it. How do we do that? It's when we receive His grace, but then choose not to walk in it. As human beings, we think we have to earn what we have, so instead of walking in His grace, we try to do things in our own strength. That will get us things, but it won't get us the abundant life God has for us. Grace is an enablement, and we are meant to walk in it. Our part is to cooperate with it to receive the greater things of God.

An example of receiving grace in vain would be if I bought someone a week's worth of groceries and told them all they had to do was go get them, but they never did. I freely gave them the groceries, and they received them in their heart and said, "Thank you," but since there was no corresponding action (they never picked them up), my grace given was done in vain.

Grace received, but never applied (walked in), is grace received in vain. When we know where we're supposed to be and what we're supposed to be doing, then we need to, on purpose, receive and walk in His grace, so we can do it with excellence.

When we don't walk in His grace to stand against the enemy, to serve, to prosper, to live our daily lives, we are trying to do it on our own. It's very easy for all of us to slip back into wanting to make things happen, but if we don't walk in His grace, we will not see the victory. Our faith must receive this grace, and then by grace we walk in the finished work of Jesus Christ. I can receive my healing and be healed because it's finished. I can receive my blessing and be blessed because it's finished. I can receive protection and be safe because it's finished. It's done. Jesus already did it. That's why Jesus is sitting down in heaven next to the Father because it is finished!

I learned about accessing His grace early on before I ever entered the ministry. When God led me to go to Bible School in Oklahoma, I quit my accounting job, and then got another accounting job in Oklahoma to pay my way through school, but it wasn't where God told me to work. Because I had disobeyed God and wasn't where I was supposed to be, there was no grace for me to do my new accounting job. I made more mistakes in one week than I had in my entire accounting career back home, so I quit before I got fired, and obeyed God by becoming a manager at the golden arches of McDonald's. And because I was now where I was supposed to be, I had God's grace to walk in, which enabled me to manage with excellence and turn a poor performing store into one of the best. God used those two years at McDonald's to teach and train me in faith and about working with and helping people. Each day I would believe for what the sales amount would be, and we would meet it. During my commute to work, I grew in my ability to speak in psalms and hymns and spiritual songs. The Lord had said that if I didn't work at McDonald's, I would miss half my training for the ministry. Looking back, I am so glad I obeyed, because much of how I do things today is because of what I learned while working at McDonald's. The point is, even though it was a secular job, the grace was there for me to do it with excellence.

Now that I'm in the ministry, the grace is there for me to pastor, and His grace has caused me to labor even more abundantly as the Apostle Paul said.

> *1 Corinthians 15:1, But by the grace of God I am what I am: and his grace which was bestowed upon me was not in vain; but I laboured more abundantly than they all: yet not I, but the grace of God which was with me.*

God's grace empowers and enables us to labor in His strength and ability in all that we do, so we can finish our course with joy. God doesn't want anyone to become stagnant. His will for us is to continually grow in His grace and ability, so we can increase in what we do and in what we have. We can only do that when we receive His grace, by faith, and walk in it. Believers who are not growing in their knowledge of and obedience to Him, are receiving His grace in vain.

2. Do not frustrate God's grace.

Galatians 2:20-21

[20] I am crucified with Christ: nevertheless I live; yet not I, but Christ liveth in me: and the life which I now live in the flesh I live by the faith of the Son of God, who loved me, and gave himself for me.

[21] I do not frustrate the grace of God: for if righteousness come by the law, then Christ is dead in vain.

These verses deal with saving grace but apply to all the graces. Paul was talking to the believers in Galatia, who had gone back to trying to earn their righteousness. He even called them "Foolish" because they were frustrating the grace of God. Righteousness is not of the flesh, so it cannot be earned. Righteousness is of the spirit, so it must be received.

I like the way the Amplified puts it.

Galatians 2:21 (AMP) I do not ignore or nullify

202

*the [gracious gift of the] grace of God [His
amazing, unmerited favor], for if
righteousness comes through [observing] the
Law, then Christ died needlessly. [His suffering
and death would have had no purpose
whatsoever.]"*

Paul said, he did not ignore or nullify the grace of God. In the Old Testament, they only had the law, with its rules and regulations, which they could never fulfill. Today, so many people are still trying to earn their righteousness and the things of God through good works, but the Holy Ghost came to reprove the world of sin, righteousness, and judgment (John 16:8). What does it mean to reprove? It means to give correction, and in this case, correcting religious teachings that say, "By our good works we can be saved." Those who have come from this type of background need to learn that Jesus, who knew no sin, became sin, so we could become righteous. That means, once we are born again, we are now the righteousness of God in Christ Jesus (2 Corinthians 5:21). When we know and understand that we are already righteous, it will keep us from becoming works minded in our faith walk. Now that Jesus has come, we are no longer under the law, but under the Spirit of life in Christ Jesus (Romans 8:2), which has made us righteous. We will never be more righteous than we were the day we accepted Jesus. So, anyone born again, who is still trying to earn their righteousness, can stop, because it's something we have already been freely given.

How else do we frustrate the grace of God? Any time we try to receive the things of God by doing in our own strength, we have frustrated the grace of God.

If you feel people are disappointing you, it's probably because you're relying on them and not God. That's an easy fix. Just get your eyes back on Jesus. We will always have problems to deal with, but God chose you for the place you are in because He knew, by His grace, you could do it.

If you feel pressured or don't think things are coming together as they should, it's probably because you're trying to make things happen. I have to be especially careful of this one, because I like to get things done, not only for myself but to see those around me get things done too, so it's easy for me to try and make things happen. Whenever there is no power in what I'm doing, or it doesn't seem to be working, I immediately know I've stopped walking in His grace and am trying to do it on my own. If I want God's highest and best in all that He has promised, I have to stop trying to make things happen, because I can't make God do anything. This is easier said than done. I remember when I was believing for our new church building. The money needed to complete the building and equip it caused me to get under so much pressure that I began to work my faith by doing everything I knew to do to get God to move. I would confess the Word, fast a little, and do anything else that came to mind. Then, one day, as I was ministering to the Lord, He asked me a question. I've since learned that when the Lord asks a question, even if I think I know the answer, I really don't. He asked, "Mark, does your faith move me?" I thought, "Does my faith move you?" Back then, I was sure I knew the answer, so I said, "Yes, Lord, my faith moves you." Then He said, "Mark, I don't need your faith to move me. I've already been moved. I need your faith to receive from me." What God said caused me to see that I had gotten out of grace and was trying to make things happen, so I repositioned myself, and, by faith, received the new building and counted it done. I knew God had told me to build it, so my part was to trust Him and walk in His grace, by following the leadings of the Holy Ghost and letting Him get it done. I did, and He did; and, by the grace of God, we were able to move into our new, fully equipped building.

God has already done all He is ever going to do. Our part is to receive, by faith, all that God has already provided, and then, by His grace, walk it out. Walking in His grace isn't always easy but without it, what God has called us to do would be impossible. Knowing I was called to pastor, I started a church where God had directed me to be. At the beginning, by the grace of God, I led the praise and worship because we didn't have a worship leader yet. Then, when I got married, I wanted my wife, who is a worshipper with a great singing voice, to be the worship leader, but the Lord wouldn't let me put her in charge. God still wanted me to do it. Now, I love to worship, and even though I'm not the best singer, we still had some amazing times in God, because the anointing was there. I remember this one Sunday, I was really struggling as I led praise and worship. It just wasn't good. After church, I said to my wife, "I think the grace to lead praise and worship has lifted." That's all I said. The next Sunday, leading praise and worship was a train wreck. Nothing went right, and I couldn't understand what had happened. After the service, I asked the Lord, "Where were you?" He said to me, "What could I do? You said the grace was gone." Lesson learned. I've never said that again. Don't ever talk bad about your grace even on days when it may seem hard. Don't ever despise it. Don't ever belittle it. Anything that God has done and given us should be greatly esteemed. I immediately changed my tune, repented, and accessed the grace again to lead praise and worship and the anointing returned. Our words about His grace will determine where we go. Our words can be stout against us, or they can be for us. Don't ever talk against the grace; because when you do, you have nullified the grace of God, which causes His grace to stop operating in your life.

It's also true that when we don't let the grace of God flow

in our lives, we've gone back into works. So, to frustrate God's grace is saying, "His grace has become meaningless," because we are trying to do it in the flesh, instead of walking in the grace that He has made available for us. We can all tell when we're walking in the flesh, because things get harder and we become weary; but when we walk in the spirit of grace, we are enabled and desire to do more. For me, the grace on my life causes me to want to teach the sheep, minister to the broken hearted, lay hands on the sick, and it also gives me a bigger heart for the lost and the backslidden, so let's receive and walk in His grace, because that is God's highest and best.

You know His voice, so if you're in the right place, but you're frustrated, then you are probably frustrating the grace of God on your life. Only you and God know, so pray and seek God, so you can be sure of your calling like I did when I started the church. Then, make sure you're not trying to make things happen in your own strength.

I want to challenge every person reading this book to receive all of His grace. Choose to go higher and don't settle when you know God has more for you. This is especially important to those pastors who say, "I'm just fine with the small church I have." Having a small church is great if that's what God has told them to do, but if they know God has called them to do more, they shouldn't stop just because they are comfortable with what they have. This is hindering His grace and could stop the flow of God's grace in their life. God loves people, and there are so many that need to be saved, filled with the Holy Ghost, healed, and discipled. This is the season of harvest and there is such a grace available for us to bring in that harvest. It is a big job, but God is not asking us to do it on our own. He's asking us to do it in His grace. Receive His grace and walk in it because it's the grace in your life that will bring in His harvest and reach the nations of the world.

To pastors who say, "I'm trying to grow my church," I would say, "Stop trying to grow it yourself, and just let the grace of God that's in you grow it." God has put the grace and ability in you to do it, but you must access it through faith. Start accessing it today, so God's grace won't be in vain.

In 1 Corinthians 15:10, Paul said that the grace bestowed on him was not in vain, and that he labored even more abundantly because of the grace. We need His grace because ministry is a lot of work. Many people think they could become a pastor because it looks so easy; just preach once a week and you're done. They say that because they don't understand all that it takes to do ministry and that God doesn't grace everyone to be a pastor. It's only those who are called by God to pastor, who are able to access this grace. Just like God called the Apostle Paul to the Gentiles, God calls those who are to pastor; and then, gives them the ability to serve the people, the city, and the nation in which they are in. This does involve labor, but that doesn't mean doing it in our own strength or going to conferences to see how other churches are doing it. A pastor is to labor by praying and asking the Lord what to do, and then doing what He says; and when they do that, they can believe for and receive the grace God has for them to see it come to pass. That's how I do it. I pray until I hear from God and then, do what He says. I let God show me the path for this church. It's the only way to have a supernatural church and flow in the gifts of the spirit.

When we are obeying God, grace can increase and be multiplied (2 Peter 1:2). This means we can believe for the double in our church, but what I think a lot of pastors do is they believe for the outward workings, such as church doubling, finances doubling, and so on. We all want that, but let's believe for the grace to increase, because when the grace doubles, so will everything else. Seeing the double manifest is all about trusting and walking in the grace in your life and letting it multiply the church.

Growing a church starts with us growing in faith to receive more grace, so we can labor from that place of grace and not from the works of our flesh. It's about growing the church by His grace and not on our personality, because it's not about us. It's all about Him and growing His kingdom.

How can we receive the double?

> Prayer: "Father God, I ask you to double the grace on my life. You said you would multiply grace according to knowledge, so I ask for increased knowledge and revelation concerning all the graces you have made available to me, in Jesus' name. Amen!"

then believe you have received it and say …

> Confess: "I believe that the grace on my life doubles. It multiplies! Hallelujah!"

3. **Do not fall from God's grace.**

> *Galatians 5:4 Christ is become of no effect unto you, whosoever of you are justified by the law; ye are fallen from grace.*

The Galatians had fallen from grace, because of going back to performing their religious traditions and obeying all the ordinances.

The Good News Bible says, "You're outside of God's grace;" New Living says, "You have fallen away from God's grace;" and The Message says, "You fall out of grace." So, we can fall out of grace when we start trying to do it on our own. I've watched this happen to people around me. No matter how someone begins in their walk with God, if they're not taught about grace and the finished work of Jesus Christ, they will fall back into doing good works to earn the things of God, instead of walking by faith. This scripture says that when someone does that, they have fallen from grace, because God's grace is no longer working in them.

Romans 6:14 says, "For sin shall not have dominion over you: for ye are not under the law, but under grace." Some will misuse this and say, "Well, we're not under the law anymore, so I'm free to do whatever I want." It's true that we're not under the religious laws (doctrines of men and their rules and regulations) or works (trying to do it on our own), but we're not free to do whatever we want, because we are still under God's laws, such as the law of love and the law of faith. If we don't walk in the law of love, we're not going to be able to apply the law of faith. What is a law? It is how something works. Gravity is a natural law, and love and faith are spiritual laws, and they always work, so to not follow them, will cause us to fall.

Religion and traditions of men will hinder:

> *Colossians 2:8 Beware lest any man spoil you through philosophy and vain deceit, after the tradition of men, after the rudiments of the world, and not after Christ.*

In the book of Mark, the Pharisees and Sadducees were upset with the apostles, because they weren't following religious traditions, like ceremonial washings, so when they cornered Jesus about it, He said, "Because of their traditions they were making the Word of God of no effect" (Mark 7:13). When someone is operating out of tradition, religion, or works, instead of faith, they can't receive what God offers, which causes them to become very frustrated because they know all that salvation has provided, but they can never seem to experience it. Some of the most frustrated people I know are people who know what the Word of God says but cannot receive it. It's not enough to know what it says, we've got to believe it, talk it, and then do it. Grace has offered all that God is to us, but it's through faith that we receive it; so, we have to make sure we don't get off into tradition and make this a "works," or a "you owe me" program.

We have to do things according to the Bible, and not according to traditions, because victory can only come by the spirit, not by the flesh. When the Galatians were trying to turn the things of the spirit into a works program, Paul said to them, "Are ye so foolish? Having begun in the Spirit, are ye now made perfect by the flesh?" (Galatians 3:3).

When we confess the Word that we believe, we are releasing our faith, but confession was never meant to be a works program. We can't get grace to work just because we say something a hundred times, or just by being a Polly-parrot and repeating words we've heard. It's okay to start with repeating what we've read in the

Word or heard, because when we continuously confess the Word, it goes from our heads into our hearts, and then when it's in our hearts, it becomes a confession of faith. God's promises are accessed by grace, through faith, so we have to hook our heart up and believe what we confess. When we do, it will bring the desired result. We are not confessing to earn something. We are confessing because we believe something, so Jesus can be the high priest over the Word we have spoken and can bring it to pass. If we have no profession (confession) of our faith (Hebrews 10:23), Jesus doesn't have anything to be the high priest over. We can't be saved without confession, and we can't receive anything from God without it.

4. Do not fail God's grace.

> *Hebrews 12:15 Looking diligently lest <u>any man</u>*
> <u>*fail of the grace of God*</u>*; lest any root of*
> *bitterness springing up trouble you, and thereby*
> *many be defiled.*

This verse is talking about living grace and says we can "fail of the grace of God" and have a "root of bitterness" spring up in us. How does someone get a root of bitterness? It starts when something happens, and we won't forgive the person who did it. Instead of receiving God's grace to forgive them, we hold on to the offense and have failed of the grace of God. The grace was there, but we failed to use it.

213

When we choose to keep this weed of unforgiveness, it will take root in our heart, and then spring up into a full plant of bitterness. It's not hard to tell when someone has done this, because all they want to talk about is the offense; but when they do that, they can defile those who listen to their offense. The word "defile" is the same meaning as the word "rape." It means to morally contaminate the innocent. In telling others about their offense, it can cause the listener to pick up their offense. How? It can be as simple as someone siding with the person offended or giving them a thumbs up on Facebook. It's just agreeing with someone's bitterness and joining in. So now, this same root of bitterness will begin to grow in the person they told, but this person who picked up their offense doesn't have the grace to let it go, because it was not their offense. That's not to say they can't get rid of it, but it will be harder to get it fully gone because there is no grace available for them to do that.

How can we avoid a root of bitterness? We need to remind ourselves that their bitterness doesn't belong to us, so don't take it. Just love them and help them with the Word, when possible, and then walk away and pray that they will come to their senses and obey the Word of God.

We cannot afford to have a root of bitter because of unforgiveness, or let it defile others. We just don't have time for it because it will get us off course from the plan God has for our lives. We must determine that when an offense comes, we will quickly forgive and by His grace, let it go, so we will not fail of the grace of God.

Jesus talked about unforgiveness.

> *Mark 11:25 And when ye stand praying, forgive,*
> *if ye have ought against any: that your Father*
> *also which is in heaven may forgive you your*
> *trespasses.*

Jesus said to forgive. Why? Because Jesus knew if we allow a root of bitterness to grow in us, our faith won't work.

I have discovered that "unforgiveness" and "not walking in love" are two of the most used tools by the devil. When the devil sees somebody doing us wrong, immediately he will amplify it by bringing bad thoughts to us about why we shouldn't forgive them. If we give in to what the enemy is saying, we are allowing a root of bitterness to be planted and grow in our heart. For a plant to live, the first thing a seed does, whether it's a good plant or a weed, is put down roots. Then, when the roots get strong, the plant will grow strong. That's why we can't listen to the enemy and allow any bitter seeds to get in us. We must obey God and stay strong by choosing to forgive, so offenses can't form a root of bitterness in us!

Those who say, "I just can't forgive them," have failed to receive the grace of God to enable them to do it. We should always forgive, but our soul (mind, will and emotions) doesn't want to, and that is the reason we need to be led by our spirit, so we will forgive. There are times I would rather slap someone upside the head, but that would be allowing my flesh to rule, and it certainly would not be walking in love. God commanded us to love others, and love forgives, thinks the best of others, and does so much more (1 Corinthians 13 AMPC).

What is the devil trying to do morning, noon, and night? To get us offended, so we'll stop loving others, because he knows that faith works by love (Galatians 5:6). He not only wants you to get upset with family, friends and brothers and sisters in the Lord, but he especially wants you to get upset with the harvest (unbelievers in the world). Why? Because he knows if we're upset with them, we won't reach out to them. We have to remember that their wrong actions are because they are not born again, and they are just acting out of their flesh, so we shouldn't get mad at them for it. We were once like them, until we were born again and received our new nature; then, as we renewed our mind with the Word of God, we were able to think, talk, and act like God. The only chance for an unbeliever, is for us to love and pray for them, and tell them the truth from the Word of God, so they too can be born again, and then, get into a good Bible teaching church where they can be discipled.

Jesus commanded us to love one another, and that means everyone, and not just the ones we like. We are to love the unlovely, which includes those not born again. We are to love our brothers and sisters in the Lord, even when they act unlovely. Even when someone irritates us to where we want to wring their neck, just love them anyway and watch the devil get mad, because instead of becoming bitter, we have chosen to walk in love. That's how loving someone works; as we love others, the grace on our life will increase, and we and our family will be blessed. It's when we choose to talk and act like the world, that God's grace is shut off in our life, because it will not operate when we walk in the ways of the world instead of God's ways, so let's not let that happen to us.

Whenever you start to feel offended, deal with it immediately, and say, "Lord, on purpose, I receive your grace to forgive them." When you say that and mean it, His grace will immediately kick in, so you can do it. Even if you have to forgive them every day, every hour, or every minute for an offense, in time, you will get to the place where you have truly forgiven them and have let it go. There will always be things happening that could offend us, but we must refuse to take the offense; instead, we must choose to walk in love by forgiving the offense, because when we do that, we will not fail of the grace of God.

How do we know when we have forgiven someone? Because when someone or something reminds us of the offense, it will no longer bother, upset, or anger us. We may still remember it historically, that it factually happened, but we will no longer become emotional about it, because we have forgiven them and let it go.

The devil wants us to keep the offense and other people's offenses too, so a root of bitterness will grow in us; but when we choose to forgive, no one will be defiled, because that root of bitterness was never planted in our heart. God has forgiven us of our sins, and we should, by His grace, forgive others. It's the same grace that forgave us, that we can access to forgive others. Even though God has given us everything, including grace to forgive, there are times when we still disobey and do our own thing. I'm so glad that when that happens, we too can be forgiven (1 John 1:9) when we come to our senses.

Forgiving an offense is so much better than holding on to it. Letting it go will keep us from crying over it, or needing a punching bag to release our anger, or replaying it over and over in our mind. In the gospels, when they ran out of wine, the mother of Jesus told the servants, "Do what He says." That's what we all need to do when an offense comes. Just do what Jesus said and forgive, so it won't hinder your faith walk.

5. <u>Do not insult God's grace.</u>

Jude 1:4 (NLT) I say this because some ungodly people have wormed their way into your churches, saying that God's marvelous grace allows us to live immoral lives.

The condemnation of such people was recorded long ago, for they have denied our only Master and Lord, Jesus Christ.

Let's look at that same verse amplified.

Jude 1:4 (AMPC) For certain men have crept in stealthily [gaining entrance secretly by a side door]. Their doom was predicted long ago, ungodly (impious, profane) persons who pervert the grace (the spiritual blessing and favor) of our God into lawlessness and wantonness and immorality, and disown and deny our sole Master and Lord, Jesus Christ (the Messiah, the Anointed One).

This is talking about men who took the message of grace and twisted it to their own advantage. They perverted it by teaching others that God didn't care what they did, which led believers into lewdness and sexual sin. This was a false teaching because God cares about everything we do. That's why He gave us grace, so we could live a righteous and victorious life!

God's grace is His ability, His favor offered to us, so let's not get into the habit of ignoring it because that would be insulting the Spirit of grace. God is offering all that He is, which in the Old Testament, before Jesus came, was done by the law, but with it came judgment, because the law could never be fulfilled. Now Jesus is saying, "I've

219

come and given you all that I am. You are no longer under the law of rules and regulations, but under the Spirit of Life in Christ Jesus (Romans 8:2), so walk in My grace."

How else can we insult God's grace? By turning it into lasciviousness and an excuse to sin. What is lasciviousness? It is wild, unrestrained living. It's someone who says, "God made me this way; and by the grace of God, I am what I am, so that's why I do what I do." They have misinterpreted 1 Corinthians 15:10 that says, "But by the grace of God I am what I am," which is talking about serving grace, who God has made us to be and what He has called us to do. It is not saying we can do whatever we want to do. God's grace is not given to anyone so they can sin. God doesn't wink and nod at sin. Now, some in the body of Christ may do that and say it's okay, but it'll never be okay with God. God's grace is so we can live free from sin. When we use God's grace as an excuse to sin, we are turning His grace into lasciviousness.

When people live in lasciviousness, doing whatever they want to do, and say, "It doesn't matter because God's grace will cover it," they are self-deceived, because that's not in the Bible. People who think that way are not walking in the spirit of His grace but are walking in their flesh. When we truly walk in His grace, it will empower us not to sin or live a lascivious life.

220

What does the Bible say about living a lustful life?

Hebrews 10:26-29 (AMP)

[26] For if we go on willfully and deliberately sinning after receiving the knowledge of the truth, there no longer remains a sacrifice [to atone] for our sins [that is, no further offering to anticipate],

[27] but a kind of awful and terrifying expectation of [divine] judgment and the fury of a fire and burning wrath which will consume the adversaries [those who put themselves in opposition to God].

[28] Anyone who has ignored and set aside the Law of Moses is put to death without mercy on the testimony of two or three witnesses.

[29] How much greater punishment do you think he will deserve who has rejected and <u>trampled under foot the Son of God</u>, and has considered unclean and common the blood of the covenant that sanctified him, and has insulted the Spirit of grace [who imparts the unmerited favor and blessing of God]?

This was written to believers who were not walking in the light of what they knew, and were continuing to sin by committing adultery, stealing, lying, and so on, thereby insulting the grace of God. Verse 29 says they have "trampled underfoot the Son of God."

Besides living a lascivious life and willfully sinning, how else can we insult God's grace? By starting out in His grace, but then relying on our own strength to make things happen. An example would be of someone starting a business because God led them to do it. They opened the business by walking in His grace, but then when things got going good, they began doing it in their own strength. Opening a business was God's calling for their life, but instead of continuing to walk in God's grace, His empowerment to run it, they chose to run it on their own. This is not only insulting God's grace, but also belittling it. The end result of not doing it in His grace could be a very tired, overworked, and frustrated business owner, and perhaps even a failed business. That was never God's intent. His plan was for them to run this business by accessing His grace and following the leadings of the Holy Ghost, so they would have a growing, successful business.

The Holy Ghost wants us to see the importance of grace, how to cooperate with it, and how to walk in it, so we can boldly say, "I will not receive the grace of God in vain. I will not frustrate the grace of God. I will not fall from grace. I will not fail the grace of God, and I will never insult the Spirit of grace." We have to make sure we are esteeming His grace, so we can walk in it.

Chapter 09

GRACE ENCOURAGEMENTS

Finally, I want to leave you with some encouraging scriptures on grace.

1. <u>We can grow in grace</u>

> *2 Peter 3:18 (NKJV) But grow in grace and knowledge of our Lord and Savior Jesus Christ...*

We can all grow in grace and in the knowledge of Jesus Christ. That encourages me! Hosea 4:6 says, "My people perish for a lack of knowledge," or it could be said, "My people perish because they don't get knowledge of the grace of God." As we grow in the knowledge of Him, we will also grow in the knowledge of grace.

We grow in the knowledge of Jesus the same way we grow in the knowledge of grace, by getting into the Word of God, looking up scriptures on both, and then meditating on and speaking them.

2. <u>Grace can be multiplied by knowledge</u>

> *2 Peter 1:2 (NKJV) Grace and peace be*
> *multiplied to you in the knowledge of God and*
> *of Jesus our Lord.*

Multiplication is good! God's grace can be multiplied in every area of our life as we grow in the knowledge of God, Jesus, and His grace. Believe for and receive more grace in your life.

Pray: "Father God, You said You would multiply grace according to knowledge, so I ask You to increase my knowledge and revelation of You and Your graces."

Confession: "I receive Your grace and I believe it multiplies in my life!"

3. <u>We can access grace by faith</u>

> *Romans 5:1-2 (NKJV)*
>
> *[1] Therefore having been justified by faith, we*

> *have peace with God through our Lord Jesus Christ,*
>
> [2] *through whom also we have access by faith into this grace in which we stand, and rejoice in hope of the glory of God.*

This scripture is talking about standing grace but applies to all graces. We can only access grace through faith, and faith comes by hearing the Word of God (Romans 10:17). The grace we currently walk in, is in direct proportion to what we believe (Romans 12:6). So, the more faith we have, the more grace we can obtain. When we believe God's Word and speak and act on it, we will see His promises come to pass in our life.

I remember a time when I needed to access more grace. It was after I came back to the Lord and realized I was called to the ministry. My pastor asked me to preach on a Wednesday night. I had never preached before and was limited in what I knew, but the Lord had given me Luke 4:18-19 to preach, which starts out by saying "The Spirit of the Lord is upon me because He has anointed me to preach the gospel," so I had my message ready. I thought my pastor would be out of town when I preached, but when I got to the church that night, he was there. I told him I couldn't preach in front of him, but he said, "Just get up there and give what you've got." Right then, the devil jumped on my shoulder and reminded me of my stammering lips and trembling legs that I would get in speech class in my senior year of high school. I would get so nervous when I had to speak in front of people. Instead of listening to what the enemy was saying, I started thinking about how merciful and kind the Lord is, and how the Spirit of the Lord was upon me. I did that without really knowing what I was doing, and by faith, I tapped into the grace that was on my life. I still remember taking those two scriptures and preaching for 45 minutes while barely looking at my notes because God's grace was there for me, and it can be there for all of us when we tap into His amazing grace by faith.

4. <u>Grace is given to the humble</u>

> *James. 4:6 ... God resisteth the proud, but giveth grace <u>unto the humble</u>.*

> *1 Peter 5:5 (NKJV) Likewise you younger people, submit yourselves to your elders. Yes, all of you be submissive to one another, and be clothed with humility, for "<u>God resists the proud, But gives grace to the humble</u>."*

These two scriptures connect grace with humility. His grace can only be received through faith when we humble ourselves and fully come under His lordship.

> *1 Peter 5:6 Humble yourselves therefore under the mighty hand of God, that he may exalt you in due time.*

In ourselves, we aren't big enough or bad enough to take on the devil. We need God's grace to do that, so we can resist the enemy and walk in victory; but receiving this grace requires us to be humble

What does it mean to be humble? It doesn't mean acting worthless. It's not weakness, but a strength. It's someone who knows they can't do what God has called them to do on their own (John 15:5), but they can do all things in Him (Philippians 4:13). When we can say from our heart, "I've been made righteous <u>in Him</u>, I'm accepted <u>in Him</u>, and I can know all things <u>through Him</u>," that is truly being humble.

Humility is so important, because God resists the proud, and we certainly don't want Him resisting us.

Where does humility start?

James 4:7-9

[7] <u>Submit yourselves therefore to God</u>. Resist the devil, and he will flee from you.

[8] <u>Draw nigh to God</u>, and he will draw nigh to you. <u>Cleanse your hands</u>, ye sinners; and purify your hearts, ye double minded.

[9] <u>Be afflicted, and mourn, and weep</u>: let your laughter be turned to mourning, and your joy to heaviness.

These scriptures tell us:

- Submit ourselves to God.
- Draw near to God.
- Cleanse our hands.
- Be afflicted, mourn and weep.

Now, don't let the last one mess with you. To be "afflicted, and mourn, and weep," is not talking to those believers who are walking uprightly before God, but to those who are living in and practicing sin. When someone is living like that, they shouldn't be happy, but should be mourning and weeping, because they are yielding to the devil. When a believer is living in sin, they don't have any grace to walk in until they repent (1 John 1:9).

It's not the Lord's job to humble us, and no one can do it for us. We have to humble ourselves. When we are truly humble, that's when we can really see that God is smarter than we are. When God calls us, "My little children," it's because we are, and still have much to learn.

5. <u>Grace is found in His presence</u>

Hebrews 4:16 (NKJV) Let us therefore come boldly unto the throne of grace, that we may obtain mercy, and find grace to help in time of need.

Paul, by the Holy Ghost, is saying that we can go, without hesitation, to the throne, and receive mercy and find grace. Whatever we need, God has it, because His grace is our answer. His grace is the fix for whatever we need fixed. God wants us to come. We are not to come weak and wimpy, or begging, and we definitely won't come if we feel unworthy or condemned. We are to come boldly. It's interesting to me that when we go to His throne and say, "God, I need help," He gives us mercy, but what He really wants us to find is His grace. Then we are to take that grace and apply it to our lives. That's how good God is.

In this scripture, it says, "Come boldly," but in the last scripture, it said we are to "Humble ourselves." That means, we can be humble and bold at the same time! Humility isn't being mousy or getting walked on. It's being fully dependent on God. God calls us to humble ourselves and depend only on Him; and because our confidence is in Him, He also wants us to come boldly before Him! And because we have been made righteous by the blood of Jesus, we can come into His presence anytime we want. The throne of grace is God's distribution center. There are so many things God would like to get to us, but we have to go to His throne room to receive them. God's mercies are new every morning, but we still have to come into His presence to receive and walk in those new mercies.

6. We can be strong in grace

2 Timothy 2:1 (NKJV) You therefore, my son, be strong in the grace that is in Christ Jesus.

This scripture has to do with serving grace, and we are told to be strong in this grace. It's not being strong in our own strength, but in His strength. It's not by our will power, it's by God's power. There are things we do that can be hard at times, but it gets a lot easier when we tap into God's grace and His strength to do them.

7. Great grace is available to us

Acts 4:33 (NKJV) And with great power gave the apostles witness of the resurrection of the Lord Jesus: and great grace was upon them all.

What is the resurrection? It's when Jesus was raised from the dead, and it's when we were raised up too, so we could sit in heaven with Christ Jesus. Grace has been given to us to be witnesses of the resurrection; and we do that by telling others who Jesus is and what He's done. Jesus went about doing good and healing all that were oppressed of the devil (Acts 10:38), and we can do the same! When the apostles gave witness of the resurrection, great grace was upon them, and it was so powerful that it led to the miraculous happenings in the Book of Acts. That same grace can be on us when we give witness of the resurrection; the Holy Ghost can demonstrate His power as He did when Jesus walked on the earth and when the apostles gave witness. This tells me that when signs, wonders and miracles are happening, there is an extra dose of grace that is poured out. I believe we ought to get to the place, as we give witnesses to the resurrection, that we are regularly tapping into that extra dose of grace. There's power available to do this, so we should all believe for great grace to be upon us.

When we believe for this greater dose of grace, it brings forth the power of God in us, not only to stand against the devil and be blessed, but also to be a witness to others, so mighty miracles will be seen. As the Holy Ghost worked His power in Jesus' earthly ministry, and with the Apostles, that same power of grace will be upon us too, when we cooperate with that power. That's when the Spirit of grace will be able to confirm the Word.

Confession: "I receive your great grace to give witness to others of the resurrection of the Lord Jesus Christ"

8. <u>We can abound in this grace</u>

> *2 Corinthians 8:7 But as you abound in everything—in faith, in speech, in knowledge, in all diligence, and in your love for us—<u>see that you abound in this grace also</u>.*

We're supposed to be abounding in faith, speech,

knowledge, and diligence. And then, Paul singles out grace, saying that we need to "see to it" that we also abound in grace. "Abound" means "added to."

> *2 Corinthians 9:14 And by their prayer for you, which long after you for the <u>exceeding grace</u> of God in you.*

"Exceeding" is something that can't be measured because there's so much.

Both scriptures are talking about grace to be rich and walking in the prosperity anointing. We know this, because they are both in the section of Corinthians where Paul spent two chapters talking to the church about walking in what we would call the "prosperity anointing."

If we want to access this prosperity, grace to be rich anointing, we need to understand that it's only available by grace and not by our works. Jesus became poor so we could become rich (2 Corinthians 8:9), and abundantly rich at that. Our God is a God of more than enough!

If we had been the creator of everything, we may have made a few colors, a few varieties of fruits and vegetables, and a few species of animals, but when God creates, He does it in abundance, beyond anything we could imagine. God created more than 7,000 types of apples, 9,000 species of birds, and millions of color variations. That's the abundance of our God. He is a God of extravagance, so we can always trust that He will provide for us abundantly. This verse says that God wants us to abound in His grace to be rich, so we can give into every good work and bless others.

Steps we can take to help increase the grace on our life:

- Grow our faith by reading and studying the Word of God.
- Be obedient to His Word and the leadings of the Holy Spirit.
- Be humble under God's mighty hand.
- Go boldly to the throne room to access and receive grace by faith.

Walk in His grace and receive more grace by believing, saying, and praying.

CLOSING

I have shared with you all that God has shown me concerning grace but there is always more to learn. It is my hope and prayer that you will take what you have read, and study it out for yourselves, so you can walk in these graces that God has provided. They are waiting for you. We can always go deeper in growing in the knowledge of His graces, and my desire is that you do.

Let this be a new beginning of laying down your way of doing things and picking up His way by walking and living in the graces of God to fulfill the plan He has for your life.

I'm excited for you as you take this journey, and I would love to hear your victories as you walk in this path. Below is the church address for those who would like to share their adventures.

Cornerstone Word of Life Church
P.O. Box 642
ATTN: Grace Victories
Madison, AL. 35758

Bible Institute is a two-year school focused on teaching Biblical principles in a concentrated format. Classes are available both in-person and online.

The vision for Bible Institute is to impart revelation from the Word of God, and anointings and impartations of the Spirit of God, that will enable and equip you to accomplish all God has called you to do.

Bible Institute is divided up into 8 quarters, with the school year running from early August through the end of May. Classes take place on Sunday evenings and there are 3 classes each quarter.

For more information, please visit our website:

CWOL.ORG/BIBLE-INSTITUTE

Made in the USA
Columbia, SC
14 November 2023

26142520R00134